MIGHT
AND
RIGHT
AFTER THE
COLD WAR

MICHAEL CROMARTIE is a research fellow in Protestant stud-
ies and the director of the Evangelical Studies Project at the
Ethics and Public Policy Center in Washington, D.C. He is
co-editor, with Richard John Neuhaus, of *Piety and Politics:
Evangelicals and Fundamentalists Confront the World*, and editor
of *No Longer Exiles: The Religious New Right in American
Politics*, *Evangelicals and Foreign Policy*, and *Peace Betrayed?
Essays on Pacifism and Politics*.

MIGHT AND RIGHT AFTER THE COLD WAR

CAN FOREIGN POLICY BE MORAL?

Edited by
MICHAEL CROMARTIE

ETHICS AND PUBLIC POLICY CENTER

Library of Congress Cataloging-in-Publication Data

Might and right after the Cold War : can foreign policy be moral? / edited by Michael Cromartie.
p.   cm.
Includes bibliographical references and index.
1. United States—Foreign relations—Moral and ethical aspects.   2. United States—Foreign relations—1989–   I. Cromartie, Michael.
JX1417.M52   1993
327.73—dc20   92–46608 CIP

ISBN 0–89633–180–6 (cloth : alk. paper)

Distributed by arrangement with:

National Book Network
4720 Boston Way
Lanham, MD 20706

3 Henrietta Street
London WC2E 8LU England

All Ethics and Public Policy Center books are produced on acid-free paper. The paper used in this publication meets the minimum requirements of American National Standard for Information Sciences—Permanence of Paper for Printed Library Materials, ANSI Z39.48–1984.   ∞ ™

Ethics and Public Policy Center
1015 Fifteenth Street N.W.
Washington, D.C. 20005
(202) 682–1200

Contents

Preface

E vil still stalks the planet," former president Ronald Reagan recently proclaimed in a speech to students at Oxford University. "What I propose," he declared, "is nothing less than a human velvet glove backed by a steel fist of military force." With the collapse of Communism, the former president argued, the world faces a host of smaller, yet no less dangerous, international crises.

In this post–Cold War era, the debate over the United States' role in world affairs has raised old questions about morality and foreign policy in a new form. Should "the national interest" be our only concern in world politics, or does that concept itself derive from the exercise of moral reasoning? How do we avoid the contrary flaws of cynicism and utopianism in thinking about the relationship between traditional moral values and U.S. foreign policy in the 1990s? Policy-makers need to explore such key issues as they reevaluate the moral resources available to them when they consider conflicting policy options.

In November 1991 the Ethics and Public Policy Center assembled political scientists, foreign-policy experts, and theologians from both the evangelical Protestant and Catholic communities to discuss philosophical and theological resources that may provide guidance or "middle axioms" for policy-makers currently in the thicket of international affairs. For a day and a half the participants engaged in a lively and stimulating exchange centered around papers that addressed a wide range of issues. Alberto Coll laments the lack of attention among foreign-policy ethicists in understanding the virtue of prudence, especially among evangelical Protestants; James Finn makes a case against those who would erect a wall of separation between morality and foreign policy; and George Weigel raises some disturbing questions about the Bush administration's understanding and implementation of conventional realism. Attention was also focused on the appriopriate roles of biblical revelation, general revelation, empirical analysis, history, and human reason in developing a normative structure for evaluating foreign-policy options.

The relationship of prudence to statecraft, however, was the subject that generated the most sustained inquiry, largely because of Alberto Coll's essay. One of the four cardinal virtues, prudence is the quality of mind that Aristotle identified as "practical wisdom." It is the form of wisdom evident in the choices one makes, and the means one chooses, to achieve the goals of life—and in this context, the goals of politics. The prudent statesman is one habitually disposed to weigh the advantages and disadvantages of certain policies, to seek counsel and advice on possible outcomes of such polices, and, without making rash judgments, to reach sound conclusions about particular courses of action. According to St. Thomas Aquinas, prudence is "right reason about things to be done," and a prudent person is one who "takes counsel, judges, and commands aright." Or, as the German philosopher Josef Pieper has said, prudence is "the perfected ability to make decisions in accordance with reality."

But what does this have to do with the morality and foreign-policy debate? Simply this: all statesmen seeking justice and human rights in the international arena should strive to be genuinely prudent leaders because their actions affect the lives of so many people. "Without a prudent statesman at the helm," states Alberto Coll in his essay, "the polis [is] like a ship wildly tossed about by the waves of human passions and misdirected moral energies." And prudence requires effort and study. A fuller knowledge of the much-neglected "prudence tradition" is necessary to develop the criteria that should be employed when making decisions in the complex arena of foreign policy and international conflict. In Part II of this volume, we have included excerpts from some classic texts of Aristotle and St. Thomas Aquinas to provide readers with a clearer understanding of the true nature and significance of this critical virtue.

I would like to thank Jacqueline Stark and Dan Maclellan of the Ethics and Public Policy Center for their sage editorial advice and always timely assistance. Center interns James Warner and Derek Mogck also provided invaluable help at crucial stages along the way.

We hope this book will help to advance constructive thinking about the proper relationship of virtue, ethics, and morality to international relations and foreign affairs.

MICHAEL CROMARTIE

PART I

Might and Right

1

Prudence and Foreign Policy

Alberto R. Coll

I s biblical revelation a sufficient guide for determining and conducting American foreign policy? This question can be answered in two different ways. If it is asking whether the Bible contains all the insight and counsels necessary for good and wise government, the answer is affirmative. If, however, it is asking whether reliance on the Bible ensures good and wise government, the answer must be negative. As St. Paul reminds us, knowing what the norms are is not the most difficult aspect of ethical behavior; applying them and living them is. Evangelical Christians who piously hope that the election of Christians to public office will resolve the nation's ills should recall that Oliver Cromwell and his fellow Puritans were "biblical people" who set out to establish a "commonwealth of the saints," but their rule quickly degenerated into a tyranny under which the grossest evils flourished.

The initial assumption in this essay is that politics is a realm of moral approximations, tentative compromises, and, occa-

Alberto R. Coll is principal deputy assistant secretary of defense at the Department of Defense and has taught international law and foreign policy at the U.S. Naval War College and Georgetown University.

3

sionally, choices among lesser evils. It is not a setting in which justice and righteousness triumph in their pure forms. It is the City of Man, not the City of God, and those who refuse to acknowledge this distinction and succumb to the utopian temptation often do more harm than good. As Pascal put it, "Man is neither angel nor beast, but he who tries to act the part of the angels often winds up playing the beast." Much evil and suffering have been loosed upon the world by earnest, well-meaning revolutionaries such as Cromwell and Marx who tried to assume the role of the angels.

Another assumption is that neither biblical norms nor the possession of Christian faith are in themselves sufficient to produce good statesmanship—just as they cannot produce good nuclear engineering or good carpentry. While biblical norms inspired by faith and illumined by the wisdom of the Holy Spirit will provide an excellent foundation for statesmanship, they must be supplemented by a series of skills or habits that, in their own way, resemble those required by the engineer or the carpenter. Ancient secular and Christian thinkers called these skills "practical wisdom," which was differentiated from the "theoretical wisdom" of revelation and natural law. According to these thinkers, practical wisdom or "prudence" was needed for theoretical wisdom—which they acknowledged to be the higher form of wisdom—to bear full fruit in the realm of the practical arts. They agreed that politics, while different in some important ways from carpentry or engineering, nevertheless belonged with them in the realm of the practical arts. Politics was different because its object—to secure the conditions necessary for individuals to live the virtuous life—was more far-reaching, but it was similar because its substance was a series of mundane, day-to-day decisions and processes that they described as the "management" of the state.

This is not a view of politics with which all evangelicals, or perhaps even a majority of them, are comfortable. Many evangelicals have not relinquished the Cromwellian dream. For them, politics is a much more earnest business that involves creating the millennium on earth. Indeed, this vision, through Jonathan Edwards and others, shaped the founding of the American republic and, in a secularized version, continues to color the views of many Americans about their nation's destiny. It is difficult to fit the notions of politics as a practical art within such an eschatological and theological framework. I hope, however, to delineate the salient elements of the notion of prudence and to discuss its relevance for modern evangelical thinking about foreign policy.

Prudence as a Tradition

The notion of prudence or practical wisdom is basic to a way of thinking about the ethical dilemmas of foreign policy that can be legitimately described as a tradition. This prudence tradition has two hallmarks. First, it recognizes the considerable difficulty of translating ethical intentions and purposes into policies that will produce morally sound results. Theorists and practitioners of statecraft sometimes consider prudence to be the virtue that enables its possessor to introduce moral goals into the stubborn and less-than-hospitable realities of international politics.

As a tradition, then, prudence often has been associated with a sober reading of the human condition and its possibilities that resembles those of secular realists such as Thucydides and Niccolò Machiavelli. Unlike these realists, however, leading prudence theorists such as Aristotle, Thomas Aquinas, and Edmund Burke have refused to acquiesce in the collapse of the "is" into the "ought." While acknowledging the dark side of human nature and politics, prudence theorists have insisted on the ultimate authority of the "ought" over the "is," and on the feasibility of moral action in an admittedly recalcitrant world. Nevertheless, the philosophically conservative bent of the prudence tradition has caused it to be shunned by those traditions, religious and secular, that seek to transform radically the patterns of international politics. Radical Christian and secular millenarians, utopians, and revolutionaries have little use for prudence.

The second hallmark of the tradition is the emphasis it places on the statesman's character. Character is seen as a key component in the ability to act morally in the political world. Writers concerned with prudence argue that a statesman's religious, philosophical, or ideological views provide a less reliable indicator of his capacity for prudence than do a series of character traits and intellectual virtues. This focus on character makes the prudence tradition distinctive. While writers about prudence recognize the power of political philosophy and conceptions of morality, they affirm that the statesman's character and his habits of decision-making and action are central to the concrete fulfillment of notions of the good.

In the West, the prudence tradition has accepted the general proposition that, although politics is distinctive from morality, it is ultimately grounded in, and justified by, it. There are two major currents of dissent from this proposition with which the prudence tradition has had to contend. One—that of secular realists such as Thucydides, Machiavelli, and Thomas Hobbes—maintains that politics and morality are basically divorced and that, for the practical man of affairs, the considerations of the political realm must regularly take precedence over those of morality. Thinkers and statesmen in this camp view skeptically the Aristotelian or Thomistic claim that the morally right can be harmonized, however tentatively, with the politically good. Hence, they define prudence as a skill of discerning the course of action that best serves one's self-interest; therefore, it is unconnected to morality, which is supposedly the pure or unencumbered search for the truly good.

Aristotelian and Christian understandings of prudence differ significantly from those of secular political realism manifested by Thrasymachus in Plato's *Republic*, the Athenian spokesmen in the Melian dialogue, Machiavelli's *Prince*, and Hobbes. In this latter tradition, prudence is equated with caution, stealth, and the successful quest for survival at all costs; its guiding norm is the survival of the self or a particular political community, with few, if any, restraints on the range of means allowed for pursuing this end. By contrast, Aristotle distinguished true prudence from "shallow cleverness"; and, like him, Aquinas contrasted practical wisdom with a series of "false prudences," the most important of which is "astutia" or cunning. The false prudences exalted by the secular realists have at their root the sin of covetousness, which is an "immoderate straining for all the possessions which man thinks are needed to assure his own importance and status . . . an anxious senility, desperate self-preservation, overriding concern for confirmation and security."[1] Unlike Machiavelli, Aquinas considered moral excellence a requirement, albeit not a guarantee, of prudence.

At the opposite end of the spectrum from the secular realists stands an equally formidable group that the tradition of normative prudence has had to face. This group is composed of several religious thinkers and other idealists who agree with the prudence theorists that politics should be grounded in morality but who view prudence warily. They suspect it is a Trojan horse for the importation of potentially corrupting extraneous considerations into the citadel of biblical ethics. Whereas the secular realists deprive prudence of its richer meaning by reducing it to mere pragmatism, the more radical among the idealists view prudence as the first step down the slippery slope of allowing biblical imperatives to be subjected to politics. Interestingly, the secular realists have been so successful in expounding their particular definition of prudence that in today's philosophical and political discourse, the prudential is regularly equated with the self-interested, even by people, such as Joseph Nye, who do not share the secular realists' philosophical assumptions.

The tradition of normative, as opposed to self-interested or value-free, prudence represented by Aristotle, Aquinas, Burke, and Reinhold Niebuhr has refused to disconnect prudence from morality. It has insisted that it is possible to bridge the worlds of morality and politics and to pursue and achieve moral objectives in the political world, even if the objectives themselves must be redefined and adjusted in the process. This branch of the tradition also has maintained that whenever the intellectual skills associated with prudence are used for immoral purposes, they lose their character as attributes of prudence and become merely forms of cunning or cleverness. Prudence is not value-free; it remains under the guidance, however ambiguous or indirect, of moral principles.

"Normative prudence" is distinctive in its insistence on the connection between the spheres of politics and morality—each of which is allowed considerable space for its own inner dynamics. Attacked by moral purists, who sometimes consider it little more than an incoherent form of realism, and by secular realists, who deny the possibility of maintaining any form of harmonious tension between morality and politics, this tradition of prudence has appealed to theorists and practitioners who have sought a middle ground from which to develop a statecraft that is neither politically impractical nor morally bankrupt.

The Aristotelian Roots

Aristotle considered prudence or practical wisdom the highest form of excellence in political life. Without a prudent statesman at the helm, the polis was like a ship wildly tossed about by the waves of human passions and misdirected moral energies. Prudence manifests itself in two dimensions of statecraft—the ends and the means. It aims at choosing a good end or virtuous action, and, in so doing, it requires a capacity for deciding well—for excellence or "fitness" in the process of deliberating and choosing ends. Prudence also concerns itself with the means whereby one can attain such a good end. Thus, prudence is both a defining and an instrumental virtue. A prudent statesman must choose among competing ends; he then engages in the process of considering the means by which he will attempt to achieve the chosen end. In Aristotle's view, statesmen such as Pericles were prudent because they had "the capacity of seeing what is good for themselves and for mankind, and these are, we believe, the qualities of men capable of managing households and states."[2]

It is significant that Aristotle cited the management of "households and states" as the preeminent arena for prudence. Prudence involves managing the practical dilemmas of daily life with due regard, not only for that which is good, but also for the inherent complexities and difficulties of social and political realities. Unlike abstract speculation or theoretical wisdom, practical wisdom is concerned "with human affairs and with matters about which deliberation is possible." The realm of prudence is that of the contingent, the relative, and the uncertain; it is fraught with fluidity, ambiguity, and "might-have-been's."

At the core of prudence are a number of character traits or secondary virtues. Not everyone is equally endowed by nature with such traits, and an individual aspiring to possess them in their ripest form must cultivate them diligently so that they can become habits and an integral part of that person's character. The components of prudence are deliberateness, self-control, and good sense.

One feature of prudent persons is their ability to deliberate well. According to Aristotle, "excellence in deliberation will be correctness in assessing what is conducive to the end, concerning which practical wisdom gives a true conviction."[3] Deliberation is intrinsic to moral reasoning, and it requires a degree of existential gravity and modesty—sufficient gravity to recognize a moral dilemma when faced with one, and the modesty to acknowledge one's limitations in resolving it. The essence of deliberation is a pause and a dialogue—a pause should precede all difficult moral decisions in statecraft; the subsequent dialogue is one in which the decision-maker, having paused, engages his own conscience and that of others to wrestle with the problem. Deliberateness, like the other defining characteristics of prudence, is a practical virtue that is concerned with practical, contingent things. Politics, which is the highest realm of prudence, is also one of the highest realms for deliberation.

There can be no good statesmanship or healthy political life in a society that does not acknowledge deliberateness as a virtue and deliberation as an indispensable prerequisite to the attainment of good political ends. I would suggest that, precisely because evangelicals are vulnerable to the hubris of believing that their political biases are divinely inspired, they should reflect on the value of deliberation in political thinking and action. The evangelical tendency to view politics through the prism of prophetic judgment must be tempered by the modesty and self-questioning implicit in Aristotle's notion of deliberation.

Self-control is another component of prudence. Men are easily swayed by pleasure and pain, which tend to "destroy and pervert" our convictions "concerning how we should act." A person who has self-control, however, is aware of both his limitations and his abilities. He will withstand the swayings of pain and pleasure, and persevere in his course of action, undaunted by either passions or the shadows of the imagination. The prudent statesman knows that the achievement of good ends in statecraft is not a fully rational enterprise untroubled by uncertainties or calamities. He will expect considerable resistance and opposition, be it from individual passions or vested interests, or from the sheer chaos of social life. But the statesman will persevere and seek the most complete approximation possible between the good ends he perceives and the recalcitrant environment that perpetually confronts him.

The third character trait or habit in Aristotle's catalogue of the elements of prudence was good sense, which he equated with sympathetic understanding. Good sense has two dimensions—one is the ability to make "correct judgment of what is fair and equitable"; the other is the "sense to forgive" and put oneself in another's place. The two dimensions of sympathetic understanding are intimately related. A "correct judgment of what is fair and equitable" requires ultimately putting oneself in someone else's place. In some circumstances, such a judgment may require us to forgive.

The fairness and equity to which sympathetic understanding leads are far removed from strict legal demands that the last ounce of flesh be paid and that justice be done even if the heavens fall. As Aristotle makes clear in his discussion of equity elsewhere in the *Ethics* and the *Politics*, equity and fairness are a higher and more perfect form of justice than strict legal justice as commonly understood.[4] Equity and fairness adapt the requirements of justice to the weakness of human nature and the vagaries and ambiguities of the human condition, which is in keeping with Aristotle's concern throughout the *Ethics* to avoid building an ethical system that is oblivious to the sad realities of human existence.

Influenced by Aristotle, Edmund Burke remarked that magnanimity is the essence of political wisdom, which is a point that Lincoln would immortalize in his Second Inaugural

Address with his call for "charity for all and malice toward none." Burke was referring, not so much to the Aristotelian virtue of high-mindedness, which commentators sometimes translate as magnanimity, but to Aristotle's sympathetic understanding, which is accompanied by fairness, equity, and a judicious willingness to forgive. Some of the most durable achievements of diplomacy and statecraft have exhibited this political forgiveness.

Because its purpose is action, and action involves the knowledge of particulars, practical wisdom or prudence is more concerned with particulars than with universals. "This explains why some men who have no scientific knowledge are more adept in practical matters, especially if they have experience, than those who do have scientific knowledge."[5] Theologians and scientists of exceptional brilliance, such as Karl Barth and Albert Einstein, have been notoriously poor in their political judgments, while individuals with humbler minds but far greater practical experience have been highly effective in advancing the common good in the realm of foreign policy. The focus of practical wisdom is not so much the knowledge of generalizations, which are useful in politics only to a limited degree, as an awareness of particulars and the complex multiplicity of variables in political life. No one ever knows all these variables, but the prudent statesman tries to acquaint himself with as many particulars as are relevant to the decision he is pondering. This is one reason that experience is an essential requirement of prudence.

Experience is the ripening agent without which the skills or habits of prudence fail to blend to form the character of a prudent statesman. Experience provides intimate knowledge of the possibilities that are open to human action. An experienced statesman has seen much of what political reality can produce; therefore, he is less likely to be caught completely unaware by sudden twists in the human drama. Eschewing rigidity of mind and action, he will pursue flexible and open-ended policies. He will recognize the amorphous texture of politics for what it is, and will try to anticipate the unexpected shapes that this amorphous mass may take. Long acquaintance with particulars also will give the statesman a better sense of proportion concerning the situation he faces and the means necessary to cope with it.

A statesman does not deserve to be called prudent unless he directs his efforts to good ends. Unless virtue is his end, his actions are marked not by prudence but by little more than knavery or shallow cleverness. "A man cannot have practical wisdom unless he is good. . . . Without virtue or excellence, the eye of the soul (intelligence) does not acquire the characteristic (of practical wisdom)."[6] According to Aristotle, "A man fulfills his proper function only by way of practical wisdom and moral excellence or virtue: virtue makes us aim at the right target, and practical wisdom makes us use the right means."[7] In sum, "It is impossible to be good in the full sense of the word without practical wisdom or to be a man of practical wisdom without moral excellence or virtue."[8]

The notion of prudence as an autonomous, amoral skill in the pursuit of self-interest was alien to Aristotle. For all its remarkable independence of means, Aristotelian prudence is ultimately subject to the "theoretical wisdom" of what we might call moral philosophy and theology. The practical wisdom or prudence of the political world requires the illumination of a higher wisdom. Prudence "has no authority over theoretical wisdom or the better part of our soul [the rational element that grasps necessary and permanent truths]." Prudence "issues commands" to attain theoretical wisdom, and makes the provisions "to secure it," but "it does not issue [commands] to wisdom itself. To say the contrary would be like asserting that politics governs the gods, because it issues commands about everything in the state."[9] In Platonic language, prudence is concerned with the contingent, theoretical wisdom with the transcendent, and the latter has ultimate authority over the former.

The Thomistic Elaboration

The Aristotelian conception of prudence was attractive to Christian theologians seeking to bridge the treacherous gap between the necessities and inner logic of a fallen political world and the transcendent vision of the gospel. Aquinas incorporated prudence into the Christian moral universe as the preeminent of the four cardinal virtues, and as that virtue without which justice, courage, and self-control cannot be fulfilled. Prudence is "the perfected ability to make right decisions." Its main function "is to order things well for an end or purpose. This cannot be done aright unless the end be good, and also the means be good and adapted to the end."[10] It is an intellectual virtue insofar as it directs a person to choose the proper means to an end, but it also has the character of a moral virtue because it requires the presence of moral virtue in the will directing it to good ends.

Different kinds of prudence deal, respectively, with the good of the individual, the family, and the state. The latter, also known as political prudence, is the highest and fullest form because it concerns the common good. Like Aristotle, Aquinas made the important point that while the virtue of a good man, a good citizen, and a good ruler have common elements, they are different kinds of virtue.

Aquinas accepted the Aristotelian categories of deliberation, good sense or sympathetic understanding, and experience as components of prudence, and added several others—memory, insight or intelligence, teachableness, acumen, reasoned judgment, foresight, circumspection, and caution. Memory refers to the capacity for an "honest" or "just" memory, for recollecting our past experiences and those of others realistically, without allowing our subjective desires and illusions to warp such recollections. As Aquinas phrased it, "Prudence is engaged with contingent human doings. Here a person cannot be guided only by norms which are simply and of necessity true; he must also appreciate what happens in the majority of cases." In sum, "Our calculations about the future should be based on what has happened in the past. Accordingly, our memory of them is needed for being well-advised about the future . . . recalling many facts is required for prudence."[11]

This observation was, among others things, an implicit recognition of the value of studying history for the development of sound statecraft. Most contemporary evangelicals, who, like their secular counterparts, seem notoriously shortsighted in their historical perspective, should take note of this point. The historical fund on which evangelical political thinking, whether of the Right or the Left, seems to draw is largely limited to a post-Renaissance and enlightenment frame of reference; hence, it is infectiously progressivist and triumphalist. The Right proclaims the eventual untrammeled and uncomplicated victory of democracy and capitalism; the Left urges a radical transformation toward a more biblical society. One could argue that today there is no serious ongoing effort in Protestantism to come to terms with ancient history, with the long and often sad millennia that stretch from early Egypt to the tenth century A.D. Hence, evangelical thought has little room for necessity or tragedy, much less for the possibility that in history the recurrent and the cyclical may outweigh the novel.

Another component of prudence, according to St. Thomas, is intelligence or intuitive understanding, which he defined as "certain correct appreciation of an ultimate principle assumed as self-evident." Because "prudence is right reason in human deeds . . . its entire process derives from insight and understanding." Insight or intuitive understanding is a trait that requires development over the course of a long life rich with experience. It enables a person to connect almost intuitively ultimate principles with particular, specific ends or goals in which some approximation of those principles are realized.[12]

Yet another important element of prudence is "teachableness" or *docilitas,* which is a general attitude of openness to the insights of others. It includes a willingness to remain receptive to the infinite variety of surprises that reality may hurl against our designs and policies; it is a quality of spiritual, emotive, and intellectual flexibility and humility. St. Thomas recognized that this was a difficult quality to cultivate: "To be generously docile calls for much effort, that of a person who carefully, frequently, and respectfully attends to the teachings of men of weight, and neither neglects them out of laziness nor despises them out of pride." It was bound to be especially difficult for "rulers" or political leaders. "All the same," he said, "even people in authority ought themselves to be tractable sometimes, for in matters of prudence no one is wholly self-sufficient."[13]

Acumen or *solertia* refers to the ability to act rightly in sudden, unexpected crises, and to draw upon one's inner resources when confronted by a practical dilemma that requires immediate action. Whereas the emphasis in *docilitas* is on profiting from the experience and insight of others, *solertia* focuses on the inescapable position of immediate responsibility in which a decision-maker finds himself when he must act without the benefit of consulting others. Just as "docility disposes us to gather sound opinions from others, so acumen disposes us to make correct assessments by ourselves." Acumen "is the flair for finding the right course in sudden encounters. . . . [It] hits upon the point, not only with demonstrations [that is, intellectually], but in practical issues as well."[14]

Prudence also requires reasoned judgment, which is a quality almost indistinguishable from Aristotle's "deliberateness." The "prudent man should be a good reasoner," and his judgments should be carefully reasoned. While "understanding and reason are not distinct faculties, they take their names from distinct functions; understanding from a close insight into truth, reason from inquiry and discussion." Aquinas added that, although "reasoning works with more assurance in some other intellectual virtues, nevertheless the ability to reason well is most important for prudence, in order that general principles may be rightly applied to particular issues which are various and uncertain."[15] Human beings cannot grasp truth by simple insight because their understanding is deficient, and the contingent world is less than fully intelligible to their intellect. Indeed, moral and political matters are full of uncertainty and indeterminateness. Hence, to attain any kind of practical certitude about such matters, one must reason.

Foresight or pre-vision entails the ability to foresee, as clearly as is humanly possible, the consequences of our actions and the degree to which the particular action we are about to take will lead to the realization of our goal.[16] Foresight is essential to sound statecraft, for as Aquinas observed, the past and the immediately present are beyond our ability to alter, leaving only "those future contingencies which a man can shape to the purposes of human life" as the subject of prudence. Prudent statesmen are not solely concerned with having right intentions; they also weigh carefully the consequences of their actions.

The two other components of prudence that Aquinas underlined were circumspection and caution. Circumspection is a capacity for discerning the degree to which circumstances affect the applicability of moral principles in specific situations. Because "prudence is about individual actions . . . and these involve many factors, it may happen that a means good and suitable in the abstract becomes bad and inopportune owing to a combination of circumstances." In the same way that pre-vision or foresight looks "ahead for what is in itself suitable for a purpose," circumspection looks into whether a particular action performed on behalf of a moral principle is "opportune given the existing [present] situation."[17] A prudent statesman applies moral principles with due regard for their context. We will want to treat Canada or Yeltsin's Russia differently from Kim Il Sung's Korea or Saddam Hussein's Iraq. And our opportunities for promoting human rights worldwide will vary similarly.

This means that the process of moral reasoning engaged in by a prudent statesman is not subject to simple formulas. It is an intensely complex, undetermined, and personal process at the core of which can be great uncertainty and even existential agony. Thus, the tradition of normative prudence stands apart from various forms of moral and theological casuistry that set out to resolve an ethical dilemma definitely by enclosing it tightly within the bounds of distinguishing principles and formulas drawn from previous similar cases.

The last item in Aquinas's catalogue of the elements of prudence was caution. Indeed, most people today who use the term prudence tend to reduce it to caution, neglecting its other dimensions. President Bush's national security adviser, Brent Scowcroft, for example, seemed to mean by the word prudence little more than a great deal of caution.

Aquinas described caution as an awareness of the all-encompassing presence of evil in human affairs and of the imperative to guard against its subtle manifestations. He was no believer in the perfectibility or basic goodness of man, and had a firm theological grounding in the reality of original sin. Thus, he could write, "Prudence deals with contingent actions, in which bad may be mixed with good, as true with false . . . human deeds are multiform; rights are often entangled with wrongs, and wrongs wear the air of good." In the contingent world of politics, not all situations were morally clear-cut cases of good pitted against evil. Even the most seemingly righteous causes were often tainted by sin. Caution is a form of skeptical discernment toward earthly absolutist claims—"a necessary ingredient in prudence if right courses are to be so followed that hazards are avoided."[18] While Aquinas would applaud General Scowcroft's sober bent and his skepticism toward moralist claims from the Right or the Left, he also would warn us against reducing prudence to caution.

Like Aristotle, Aquinas believed that prudence was practical wisdom in the service of the common good: "Some men, insofar as they are good counselors in matters of warfare, or seamanship, are said to be prudent officers or pilots, but not prudent absolutely; for only those are prudent absolutely who give good counsel about what concerns man's entire life." More specifically, he argued that "perversions" of rightful systems of government, such as tyranny, ignoble oligarchy, and mobocracy, "have no part with prudence," thus suggesting that, although such regimes and their rulers may be capable of some prudent acts, it is improper to speak of them as prudent per se.[19]

The Burkean Mediation

The theological successors of Thomas Aquinas, who developed his understanding of natural law further in the realm of political theory, did not pay much attention to prudence. Such prominent theorists of international law as Francisco de Vitoria and Francisco Suarez, while highly sensitive to the problematical relationship of morality to politics, focused their efforts on an analysis of natural law, just war, the nature of the international community, and the rights of persons, but said little about either the mediating virtue of prudence or the critical importance of the prudent statesman. Among the

Renaissance humanists of the fifteenth and early sixteenth centuries, a prudence tradition with classical and Christian roots flourished, especially in writers such as Pontano and Guicciardini.[20] It was effectively eclipsed by Machiavelli, however, who collapsed prudence into an amoral skill to maximize power and political success.[21]

The tradition resurfaced vigorously with Edmund Burke, who indirectly derived many of his central philosophical assumptions from Aristotle and Aquinas through the seventeenth-century Anglican divine Richard Hooker. A practitioner more than a scholar, Burke did not treat prudence with a high degree of intellectual precision, but he clearly thought it plays a key role in the relationship of morality to statecraft: "Prudence is not only the first in rank of the virtues, political and moral, but she is the director, the regulator, the standard of them all." The foundation of prudence is the unreliability of theory, by which Burke meant all forms of intellectual speculation, as a guide to practical human action. Seizing upon Aristotle's distinction between the man with scientific knowledge and the man of experience, Burke drew a similar distinction between a theorist or professor and a statesman:

> A statesman differs from a professor in an university; the latter has only the general view of society; the former, the statesman, has a number of circumstances to combine with those general ideas, and to take into his consideration. Circumstances are infinite, are infinitely combined; are variable and transient; he who does not take them into consideration is not erroneous, but stark mad . . . metaphysically mad. A statesman, never losing sight of principles, is to be guided by circumstances; and judging contrary to the exigencies of the moment, he may ruin his country forever.[22]

Time and circumstances make a great difference in the moral appropriateness, or lack thereof, of applying a particular principle: "in every question of moral and political prudence, it is the choice of the moment which renders the measure serviceable or useless, noxious or salutary."[23] More to the point, "circumstances (which with some gentleman pass for nothing) give in reality to every political principle its distinguishing color and discriminating effect." Principles, therefore, are important, and a statesman is not to lose sight of them on his difficult journey. But prudence is essential as a mediator between general moral principles and the infinitely variable and complex circumstances to which those principles must be applied.

Burke's outline of the relationship between prudence and the moral principles it mediates is not free of problems. Aristotle and Aquinas formally subordinated prudence to morality or "theoretical wisdom," while insisting that in this world it was the highest political virtue. Burke seemed to move further, or at least less equivocally, in the direction of giving prudence full autonomy when he argued that "practical wisdom [supersedes] theoretical science whenever the two come in conflict."[24] To protect himself against Machiavellianism, Burke drew a distinction between "true prudence" ("public and enlarged prudence," which is concerned with the good of the whole and which takes a larger, long-term view of things,) and "that little, selfish, pitiful, bastard thing, which sometimes goes by the name," and which is little more than cleverness or cunning.[25]

The Burkean catalogue of character traits and habits of intellect and judgment that go along with prudence was not new. The capacity to deliberate; the exercise of self-control against the passions and delusions of the mind; a profound skepticism toward any attempt to turn theoretical conclusions or "universals" directly into policy without due regard for the friction of circumstances or "particulars"; an appreciation for the value of equity and forgiveness in making political judgments; all these were part of the inner fabric of the prudent statesman. Finally, the prudent statesman had to learn to live with ambiguity, incompleteness, and inconclusiveness. As Burke wrote, "The decisions of prudence . . . differ from those of judicature . . . almost all the former are determined on the more or less, the earlier or the later, and on a balance of advantage and inconvenience, of good and evil."[26]

It was on this last point and on the philosophical possibilities it opened that twentieth-century non-Machiavellian realists such as Hans Morgenthau, Reinhold Niebuhr, and Kenneth Thompson sought to anchor their own understanding of prudence and their adherence to the prudence tradition. Unlike E. H. Carr and the early George Kennan—both of whom erected an impenetrable barrier between morality and policy—these realists were prepared to admit that the barrier was far more porous. They agreed that the relationship between statecraft and the absolute moral law, the reality of which they recognized, was far subtler and more sophisticated than either Carr or the early Kennan supposed. Statecraft could not ignore the moral law, even if it could not follow it without the aid of prudence. It was mainly through Burke that the contemporary realists acquired the concept of prudence.

In the hands of Morgenthau, Niebuhr, and Thompson, prudence has few of its Thomistic lineaments but much that is reminiscent of Burke's emphasis on its near autonomy, his distrust of ideological abstractions and moralism, his perception of prudence as a "balance" of competing goods and lesser evils, and his sharp sense of the ambiguity and inconclusiveness at the heart of the prudential decision-making process.[27] If the contemporary realists err, they do so on the side of vagueness and imprecision about the meaning of prudence—a reflection, perhaps, of their neglect of Aquinas, whom they suspected of being excessively rationalistic and legalistic, but whose understanding of prudence could have been immensely valuable to them. Yet, it may be that the realists also shied away from Aquinas because of the latter's assumption that prudence could be harmonized consistently with good means and ends. Well aware of the twentieth century's terrible upheavals, they were far more skeptical of such a claim, and far more attuned to the possibility that less-than-good means—indeed, horrible ones—might be morally justifiable in the light of ends that were either ultimately good or at least preferable to, or less evil than, the feasible alternatives. There is little of St. Thomas's quiet moral confidence and serenity in the agonized queries of Hans Morgenthau about the inevitable evil of politics or Reinhold Niebuhr's skeptical probings of the relationship of reason to man's moral and political life.

The twentieth-century realists have rendered a signal service to the prudence tradition by bringing into it an intense, almost one-sided concern with international politics. For Aristotle, Aquinas, and Burke, statecraft meant primarily the right-ordering of the polity, and only secondarily its relationship to the vast external realm beyond. For the realists, statecraft means above all steering the ship of state through the turbulent waters of international politics at a time when, thanks to nuclear weapons and modern technology, errors in this task can have ultimate, irretrievable consequences.

Ambiguities and Criticisms

The central ambiguity in the notion of prudence is its relationship to those transcendent principles to which theoretically it remains subject even while operating with considerable freedom on the plane of day-to-day affairs. Within the Christian branch of the tradition, this ambiguity takes the form of the problematical relationship between Jesus's "radical gospel," with its seemingly uncompromising transcendent reference point, and the general tenor of prudential decision-making, which tends to revolve around, and focus on, the necessities and parameters imposed by this world. It is a problem best captured within modern Protestantism by the long debates between John Howard Yoder and Paul Ramsey. Christian thinkers have attempted to lessen this tension by writing about two forms of prudence—lower prudence and higher prudence.[28] The first kind, most evident in the Old Testament and the Pauline letters, has been appropriated by Christian realists of our own day such as Reinhold Niebuhr and Martin Wright via St. Augustine's distinction between the City of Man and the City of God. In the realm of statecraft, lower prudence focuses on modest goals, such as limited order, tranquillity, and accommodation. Its inward logic is an instrumental conception of international morality coupled with skepticism toward any radical transformational designs of world politics. Aside from its concern with limited objectives, lower prudence devotes most of its energy to the question of means, to making the inevitable struggle for power among nations less brutal and dehumanizing than it otherwise might be. Its archetypical models include Hugo Grotius's counsels to moderation in *De Iure Belli ac Pacis* (1625) and Reinhold Niebuhr's observation at the end of World War II that the highest ethical action one can expect of a state in international relations is one that is both morally good and beneficial to the state's interest.[29]

Higher prudence is more willing to take risks for the sake of exploring possibilities open to ethical action. It is, in contemporary Roman Catholic language, "a virtue infused with grace; its measure exceeds that of living merely according to reason—its measure is the mind of Christ; its purpose is not to be respectable but to be a fellow citizen of the saints and a familiar of God. . . . It springs from and lives in charity, without which one may be shrewd but cannot be prudent."[30] The limits of this higher prudence in the political realm, however, are ambiguous, as are also the boundaries between lower prudence and secular realism. At what point does higher prudence become, in Eric Voegelin's words, a radically irresponsible and unrealizable desire to "immanentize the escathon"? And where is the line that separates lower prudence from a narrow, selfish desire to protect one's self-interest without causing undue harm to others?

The most serious charge brought against the prudence tradition is that the notion of prudence itself, even the "normative prudence" of Aristotle and Aquinas, is inadequate as a guide to ethical statecraft. According to this argument, the considerable freedom that prudence arrogates to itself in its choice of both which ends are to receive greater priority at a particular moment and which means are appropriate for effecting the chosen ends translates in practice into the use of prudence as an imprecise, dangerously broad rationalization for selfish pragmatism. In the everyday run of affairs, "lower prudence" ultimately takes precedence over "higher prudence," and the prudence tradition lacks the inner intellectual and normative resources to remedy this tendency. At its best, prudence fails to give a statesman rational guidance for choosing among moral principles in specific situations; at its worst, it degenerates into an intuitionism under whose spell the grossest immoralities are condoned.

The prudence tradition has offered some tentative replies to these serious charges. Contemporary "reformist" evangelical writers on ethics and international affairs, such as James Skillen, Nicholas Wolterstorff, and Ronald Sider, tend to focus on the search for biblical principles through which statesmen might create a more humane and ethical system of international relations. They have worked to demonstrate the validity of biblical imperatives, and of hypothetical policies derived from such imperatives, in issues such as nuclear deterrence, distributive economic justice, human rights, and the environment. Interestingly, the ultimate moral ends pursued by these authors do not differ radically from those accepted by most of the theorists within the mainstream "normative prudence" tradition.

What makes the prudence tradition distinctive is its reminder that moral principles are translated into actual policies only through the mediation of a complex process in which human decision-makers play a critical role. To use Aristotelian language, theoretical wisdom does not become embodied in action except through a filtering process that includes the reason, imagination, will, choices, and particular acts of particular human beings. Moral principles are ultimately realized only in specific acts that human beings choose to perform, which is the reason that character—including the foundational predispositions, attitudes, and intellectual and moral skills and habits of the statesman—is an important focus of the prudence tradition. A set of biblical principles is not sufficient to ensure that policies founded on them will be morally sound.

Prudence can be valuable in moderating some of the worst errors to which statesmen, including those of Christian faith, are prone when they confront difficult ethical choices. The Aristotelian emphasis on self-control, deliberation, sympathetic understanding, and the value of experience and intimate acquaintance with the particular details of the problem at hand serves as a useful corrective to hubris, mean-spiritedness, self-righteousness, and the politician's tendency to give primacy to ideological abstractions over the more intractable empirical realities at the core of international relations.

Aquinas brought these Aristotelian concerns into the Christian understanding of prudence. He added others: memory, the capacity for a memory of integrity and realism; teachableness, with its emphasis on intellectual and existential openness and flexibility; acumen, focusing on the skill of acting rightly in sudden crises; and foresight, which despite its theoretical difficulties, has the salutary effect of forcing the statesman to ponder the numerous consequences that may result from his actions.

The writers on prudence also have set themselves against the notion, dear to many evangelicals, that all that is required for excellence in public service is to place a "good and decent man," or a man of Christian principles, at the helm. As experience with Neville Chamberlain and Jimmy Carter suggests, a decent man does not always make a prudent statesman. To ripen into morally sound statecraft, a person's desire to do good requires cultivating those ways of thinking and acting, those intellectual and volitional habits and skills that are associated with the concept of prudence. Yet another misguided belief, congruent with our society's technological bent, is that ethical decision-making can be systematized and fully rationalized through some form of biblical literalism. Here, too, prudence warns against the understandable but morally pernicious yearning for simplification and certainty. Given the uniqueness of every agent and every situation, and the difficulty of balancing competing ends and means, prudence reminds us that at the core of ethical decision-making is a degree of existential agony and darkness perhaps indicative of man's finiteness and of his need for transcendent grace. Such grace, in Reinhold Niebuhr's words, may "complete what even the highest human striving must leave incomplete."[31] For Niebuhr, "faith in God's forgiveness" is what ultimately "makes possible the risk of action."[32]

More directly, one can argue that the processes of moral reasoning, weighing, and balancing—as well as cultivating those inward attitudes and habits that should accompany these processes—are unavoidable for any decision-maker or thinker who, confronted with moral dilemmas in the political arena, wants to balance justly the claims of morality with those of the political world. Even for those who studiously wish to avoid the use of the term, prudence may be inescapable.

In the annals of international relations, the adjective "prudent" has been reserved for those statesman who have exercised the art of ruling with sufficient excellence to earn the gratitude of their contemporaries and posterity. Although disagreement will continue about whether Pericles, Phillip II, or Bismarck deserve this honor, a greater degree of consensus may be possible concerning Washington, Lincoln, and Churchill. These statesmen rank as among the best that humanity is capable of producing. In the context of their undeniable flaws and the titanic pressures they faced, their moral wisdom is all the more remarkable. At the core of their statecraft and their moral and political reasoning was the notion, explicitly articulated or otherwise, of prudence. In their own minds prudence, or something akin to it, rather than a single moral principle or philosophy, was the mediating process and personal virtue through which they connected the moral ends they pursued with their everyday actions and policies. To argue that prudence is meaningless, useless, or noxious requires refuting a formidable body of historical experience concerning one of the important instruments by which statesman have given substance to moral principles in the political world.

Response

Nicholas Wolterstorff

Prudence, says Alberto Coll, approvingly quoting Aquinas's definition, is "the perfected ability to make right decisions" in managing one's own life, household, or state; and right decisions are those in which moral principles are applied in such a way that no other decision one could have made would ultimately have produced a morally better result. The prudence to which Coll especially refers is the prudence of the statesman; and the heart of his paper cites Aristotle, Aquinas, and Burke to delineate the main traits of prudence in the statesman. The prudent statesman is one who can deliberate well; he possesses self-control, good sense (sympathetic understanding), memory, intelligence, teachableness, acumen, reasoned judgment, foresight, circumspection, and caution.

In addition to articulating the virtue of prudence, Coll speaks of the "prudence tradition." The main purpose of his paper is to praise this tradition and commend it to us for our approval. The prudence tradition in political thought, he says, "recognizes the difficulty of translating ethical intentions and purposes into policies that will produce morally sound results," and draws attention to the character of the statesman—specifically, his prudence—as the key component in such translation. "This focus on character," Coll contends, "makes

Nicholas Wolterstorff is the Noah Porter Professor of Philosophical Theology at Yale Divinity School and Yale University.

the prudence tradition distinctive. While writers about prudence recognize the power of political philosophy and conceptions of morality, they affirm that the statesman's character
and his habits of decision-making and action are central to the
concrete fulfillment of notions of the good."

Contrast this picture of the prudent statesman with the
picture of the good king that is found in Psalm 72:

> Give the king your justice, O God,
>   and your righteousness to a king's son.
> May he judge your people with righteousness,
>   and your poor with justice.
> May the mountains yield prosperity for the people,
>   and the hills, in righteousness.
> May he defend the cause of the poor of the people,
>   give deliverance to the needy,
>   and crush the oppressor. . . .
> In his days may righteousness flourish
>   and peace abound, until the moon is no more. . . .
>
> May all kings fall down before him,
>   all nations give him service.
> For he delivers the needy when they call,
>   the poor and those who have no helper.
> He has pity on the weak and the needy,
>   and saves the lives of the needy.
> From oppression and violence he redeems their life;
>   and precious is their blood in his sight.
> Long may he live!
>   May gold of Sheba be given to him.
> May prayer be made for him continually,
>   and blessings invoked for him all the day long.
> May there be abundance of grain in the land;
>   may it wave on the tops of the mountains;
>   may its fruit be like Lebanon;
> and may people blossom in the cities like the grass
>   of the field.

What makes this picture of the good king so different from the Aristotelian-Thomistic-Burkean picture of the prudent statesman? Anybody in the prudence tradition would insist that for someone to be a good king as thus described, he would have to be prudent. We can accept that—accept it, indeed, on two different levels. The king would have to have the perfected ability to make right decisions in managing the state; and the character traits required for that, in turn, are at least approximately those specified in Aquinas's list. Therefore, the good king will be a prudent statesman, approximately as Aquinas understands that. What, then, makes the portrait so different?

It looks so different because the portrait of the good king tells us *what the king does*; it describes the fundamental aspects of his actions and the consequences thereof. And that description is very jolting for anyone who places himself in a contemporary conservative or libertarian tradition. By contrast, the picture of the prudent statesman is purely formal.

Or, is it? Coll says that the prudence tradition has a "philosophically conservative bent"; he repeatedly cites utopians and revolutionaries as the polar others—particularly, though not only, *evangelical* utopians and revolutionaries. But how, one wonders, did he manage to pull a rabbit so large out of a hat so small? Can there not be prudent revolutionaries and prudent utopians? The assumption seems to be that revolutionaries and utopians are inherently imprudent, but why is this so? If we had before us the entire range of biographies of those engaged in one form or another of revolutionary action, would we not find, among the many imprudent ones, some very prudent ones also? Indeed, after their respective revolutions, some revolutionaries went on to become rather admirable statesmen.

I am not at all certain that I know the answer to this question; Coll may argue that I misunderstood him. I suspect, however, that the answer lies in the sorts of moral principles that Coll assumes the prudent statesman tries to apply. The three thinkers who are regarded as the founding fathers of the prudence tradition—Aristotle, Aquinas, and Burke—provide a clue. All three were relatively content with the established order within their respective societies and with the political values of those in power. They were, in effect, asking themselves this question: As one who is relatively content with the established order in my society and with the underlying values guiding that order, what traits of character should I prize in those who find themselves in political office in my society? The answer they gave was—*prudence*. I would prize someone loyal to the dominant values of my society who, on the basis of wide experience, is able to evaluate the pros and cons of the various available options and select the option that will perpetuate the basic contours of the established order.

The Vision Thing

Notice that nothing is said about the ability of the statesman to inspire the people—to create a vision. Nothing is said about the ability of the statesman to empathize with those in society who are suffering. Nothing is said about the gift of the statesman for discerning what may never be done to a human being. Nothing is said about the courage that is sometimes required to prevent such abuse.

Thomas Kuhn made a distinction in his book *The Structure of Scientific Revolutions* between *normal* science and *revolutionary* science. Suppose one adds to this a third category—*contentious* science. A science will be contentious when there is considerable controversy about its appropriate goals, methods, concepts, and so forth. One should distinguish, in wholly analogous ways, among normal, revolutionary, and contentious politics. Normal politics is directed toward preserving the established order and is conducted on the basis of the agreed values undergirding that order. If normal politics is what one wishes to promote, the statesman will take precedence over all other political actors on the scene and prudence in the statesman will be particularly prized.

Although prudence seems to be a purely formal virtue, compatible in principle with various forms of politics, it is, in fact, associated with conservative politics. There is, indeed, a tradition of political thought that emphasizes prudence, but to call that tradition prudential is misleading—though not actually mistaken. It is misleading because the emphasis on prudence is only part of the tradition, and by no means a central part. The tradition of political thought in question is the tradition that, in a situation of near consensus about fundamental values, regards the most important thing in politics as the preservation of the established order in its main contours. The tradition in question is the tradition of *normal* politics—whatever normal happens to be. To use the more customary word, it is the tradition of *realist* politics.

Sometimes, however, normal or realist politics is not what is called for—just as, sometimes, normal science is not what is called for. Sometimes politics finds itself in a contentious stage, when there is no dominant consensus on values or on whether the established order should be perpetuated. In that situation a political candidate's prudence may be deemed less important than his position on the issues under contention. And sometimes politics is, or ought to be, in a revolutionary stage. Then one looks for leaders with vision, empathy, and charisma—whether or not they happen to occupy the position of statesmen. The realist tradition sells itself as the tradition that takes seriously morality and sin; in some situations, however, to have as one's fundamental political aim the stability of the established order is to take both sin and morality very *un*seriously.

American politics today is not normal politics, nor is it

revolutionary politics; it is contentious politics. We disagree about fundamental political values. If some American politician advertises himself to me as prudent—possessing "the perfected ability to make right decisions"—I shall ask him to talk about his character later but to tell me first what he takes to be right. The tragedy of contemporary American politics is, not that we lack prudent men and women, but that our prudent men and women aim at perpetuating the established order in which they occupy positions of privilege and power. Instead of enabling and conducting the intelligent and civil debate on fundamental issues that is so desperately needed, they quell the debate and offer venom, evasion, and image instead.

What I have said in general is true for us who are Christian as well: the words and actions of Christians in the political order will differ from case to case, depending on the situation. Sometimes, though I think not very often, the main concern of Christians will be to find and support prudent statesmen whose aim is to perpetuate the established order. More often it will be to find and support prudent statesmen and stateswomen who do not seek to perpetuate the established order. And sometimes not even prudent statesmen will be the main desideratum. This is true because Christians will usually have a fundamental critique to offer of the established order.

Justice, Not Utopia

My guess is that Coll hears utopianism behind that last comment, but there is nothing at all utopian about it. This essay will close with a few words about that. Hans Morgenthau, so far as I have ever been able to discern, seemed always to think of morality along Kantian lines; when he concluded that the statesman could never have a morally good will, in the Kantian sense, he concluded that politics, or at least diplomacy, was a matter of power and not morality—as if power failed to raise moral issues. When Niebuhr concluded that the politician could not implement the Beatitudes without violating the Ten Commandments, he urged politicians and statesmen to follow the laws of the *civitas mundi* rather than the *civitas dei*, and exhorted Christians to confine their religion to lamenting the irony and tragedy of our present fallen order. A similar strategy is to be found at work among those who urge natural law rather than the gospel of Christ as the basis for politics.

The conclusions drawn do not follow. What Jesus Christ, and the Scriptures interpreted through him, ask of all who will listen is that we struggle for *shalom*; at the same time they tell us that, although our endeavors will not be in vain, we must never expect that our deeds will bring in the Kingdom of God. But what, you ask, is shalom? Jesus in his deeds and words and Scripture in its words give us clues about the nature of shalom. They do not answer all our questions by any means, but the contours are there. Central in the contours of shalom, for example, is *justice*. And one of the prominent aspects of justice is the claim that the poor have rights. This does not mean merely that society would be better without poor people or that the wealthy have duties to the poor. The poor have rights—legitimate claims. In other words, if a person does not have fair access to adequate means of sustenance, that person is morally injured.

It is incumbent upon those who have acknowledged Jesus as God's decisive Word to humanity to remind our society of this, among other things, and to urge our statesmen, businessmen, and everyone else to do whatever possible to ensure that this right is secured to people. There is nothing utopian in this; prophetic, perhaps, but not utopian. It is also true that human beings have a right not to be knocked on the head while walking on the Mall in Washington, D.C. There is nothing utopian in urging our politicians and everyone else to do what they can to secure this right. We will never completely succeed in securing either right, but that is no reason not to try. Simply because a particular right or value cannot absolutely be secured does not mean that the struggle for that right or value is utopian.

Indeed, some things that should be attempted in heaven would be calamitous to attempt in this world of sin and frailty. Utopianism tries to do such things, and it is proper to warn against it. In the struggle for justice, however, as understood in the Bible, there is nothing utopian. The fact that our struggle never ends does not suggest that we should settle for second best, be it identified as the law of the city or the world, as natural law, or as the principles of political realism. Sometimes it is not prudent statesmen but, rather, bold and visionary revolutionaries whom the times demand. The need of the hour is for courageous, charismatic men and women who say, "This must not be," and then act on their conviction. So it was in revolutionary America; so it was until recently in South Africa; so it is today in the Middle East.

Sometimes it is neither prudent statesmen nor bold revolutionaries who are required above all. The need, instead, is for gifted men and women who can articulate and debate the fundamental issues of right and good that are contested in the society. So it is in the United States today. If we do insist on prudent statecraft, however, let us set before our statesmen the biblical principles of shalom. This is the moral order, rather than the conservative principles of normal or realistic politics, that they should prudently apply. When prudence is desired, let us have prudence guided by the prophetic vision of the Scriptures rather than by the aim of conserving the values of the established order. Though tragedy and irony will remain, what we lament will then be worth lamenting.

2

Morality and Foreign Policy

James Finn

The discussion of ethics or morality in our relations with other states is a prolific cause of confusion."[1] While I completely agree with this assertion of Dean Acheson, who served admirably as Harry Truman's secretary of state, I will argue that this state of affairs should not—indeed, need not—exist. Acheson and others with similar views present a challenge to those of us who believe that morality must have a purchase on the policies of the United States, both domestic and foreign, if our American experiment is to continue. After first examining the strengths and weaknesses of their views on morality and foreign policy, as well as their causes (at least partial) and consequences, I will offer an alternative—although not a wholly original one. Finally, I will consider several current policy problems that will test whatever set of principles we bring to them.

Dean Acheson supported the statement quoted above in the following manner:

The vocabulary of morals and ethics is inadequate to discuss or test foreign policies of states. . . . What passes for ethical

James Finn is senior editor of *Freedom Review*, which is published by Freedom House in New York City.

standards for governmental policies in foreign affairs is a collection of moralisms, maxims, and slogans, which neither help nor guide, but only confuse, decisions on such complicated matters as the multilateral nuclear force, a common grain price in Europe, policy in Southeast Asia. . . .

   A good deal of trouble comes from the anthropomorphic urge to regard nations as individuals and apply to our own national conduct, for instance, the Golden Rule—even though in practice individuals rarely adopt it. The fact is that nations are not individuals; the cause and effect of their actions are wholly different; and what a government can and should do with the resources which it takes from its citizens must be governed by wholly different considerations from those which properly determine an individual's use of his own.[2]

This passage has become almost a locus classicus in the literature on ethics and foreign policy. One need attend to only a portion of the debates involving ethical considerations and major policy decisions to know that they have generated deep confusion. After reading Dean Acheson's strictures, one might legitimately conclude that he not only testified but also contributed to the confusion.

Acheson's rejection of any role for ethics in international affairs rests on two basic assumptions. First, the slogans and maxims that pass for ethical standards are inadequate for the complicated matters to which they are meant to apply. What is needed to make the appropriate decisions about matters such as military forces or grain prices in Europe is technical expertise—the judgment of those who are highly knowledgeable about such specialized subjects. Moral advice cannot provide such guidance. Second, it is inappropriate and confusing to apply to states moral standards that guide individual behavior. Nations are not individuals and should not be treated as if they were. Because their action springs from different sources, they must be judged according to different considerations.

To strengthen Acheson's challenge, I will cite two supporting voices—those of Hans Morgenthau, the renowned political theorist, and George Kennan, statesman, historian, and theorist. Hans Morgenthau stated:

> The natural aspirations proper to the political sphere—and there is no difference in kind between domestic and international politics—contravene by definition the demands of Christian ethics. No compromise is possible between the great commandment of Christian ethics, "Love Thy Neighbor as Thyself," and the great commandment of politics, "Use Thy Neighbor As a Means To The End of Thy Power." It is *a priori* impossible for political man to be at the same time a good politician—complying with the rules of political conduct—and to be a good Christian—complying with the demands of Christian ethics. In the measure that he tries to be the one he must cease to be the other.[3]

This statement is even more challenging than Acheson's, for it goes beyond the assertion that Christian ethics are inadequate or confusing when applied to international affairs to state unequivocally that Christian ethics contravene the demands of political action. Morgenthau would present to the conscientious Christian two stark choices—forgo politics or discard your conscience.

George Kennan remarked:

> The interests of a national society for which a government has to concern itself are basically those of its military security, the integrity of its political life, and the well-being of its people. These needs have no moral quality. . . . They are the unavoidable necessities of a national existence and therefore not subject to classification as either "good" or "bad."[4]

It would be foolish either to ignore or to dismiss the reflective judgments of persons as thoughtful and experienced as these three, especially if one acknowledges that they speak not only for themselves but also for a number of others who have occupied high office in the U.S. foreign-policy hierarchy—and of others who still do. We must examine these charges before we refute them—or accept them as our own. Was Acheson correct in saying that moral standards appropriate to individual behavior are not applicable to international relations? Is Morgenthau correct when he asserts that one cannot be a good politician and at the same time a good Christian? Is Kennan right when he states that the societal interests for which government is responsible have no moral quality? If personal values cannot be transferred directly to affairs of state, does it follow that the latter exist in a value-free realm?

A Christian Framework: Creation, Sin, and Redemption

Such questions can best be considered within a large framework that accommodates various avenues of investigation. One spacious framework is provided by Christianity, with its concepts of creation, sin, and redemption. I will sketch in, with large brushstrokes, some elements of those concepts.

In 1963, Pope John XXIII issued his buoyant encyclical *Pacem in Terris* in which he stated that we are all "the children and friends of God, and heirs of eternal glory." Now, as children of God we are necessarily created in his image, which gives each of us—every individual—an inviolable dignity. It means that there is a transhistorical dimension to the life of every person. As children of God, we are brothers and sisters to one another; we are members of a common family and, therefore, social by nature. We are responsible to, and for, one another. Graced with intelligence and free will, we must discern how best to live our social and political lives together.

The laws governing our behavior are to be sought, according to John XXIII, "in the nature of man, where the Father of all things wrote them. By these laws men are most admirably taught, first of all how they should conduct their mutual dealings; then how the relationships between the citizens and the public authorities of each State should be regulated; then how States should deal with one another."[5] It is through these organizations that our rights and responsibilities are, at least partially, exercised.

But, however great our patrimony and the inviolable and inalienable rights that flow from it, we are flawed by original sin. The doctrine of sin, which has anthropological support, states that we are flawed, broken, weak, fallen creatures and that nothing we do will achieve perfection. We are flawed in our intellect, in our emotions, in our desires; that flaw runs through every individual and organization and through the very heart of our moral universe. Short of the fulfillment of the Kingdom of God, we cannot expect on this earth to achieve perfect and lasting happiness, perfect and lasting peace, perfect and lasting justice. The anti-utopian and realistic streak that permeates Christianity causes us to respond rather skeptically to utopian promises.

This does not, however, amount to a counsel of despair. Redemption is ours. In Pope John's phrase, we are "heirs to eternal glory." We have a right to hope and the responsibility to act in accordance with that hope. The future, which we will help to shape, is indeterminate and open. Our decisions will affect, not only our own lives and those of our families and friends, but those of our brothers and sisters often far distant.

The Challenge Restated

Within the framework provided by these concepts, we can return to the challenge posed by those who seemingly erect a wall of separation between morality and politics—at least between morality and U.S. foreign policy. We can initiate a possible response by acknowledging that, like a number of professionals who are deeply steeped in political affairs—as actors or as theorists—they were reacting, at least in part, to those who adopt either one or both of two unfortunate approaches to political affairs. The first approach endorses the application of a personal code of morality—that is, a code meant to regulate relations among individual persons—to large-scale political matters. The second is what I have termed "the moral mustard plaster" approach to political affairs. Proponents of this approach take some code of morality— from whatever source—and apply it externally, as it were, to the political issue. Their working assumption seems to be that if one knows the proper moral response to a political issue, the proper policy will necessarily follow as though on a leash. Dean Acheson accurately diagnosed these approaches as leading to grave confusion.

In the affairs of humankind, there is, apparently, a constant temptation to exorcise power from the relations between political communities. Some people who reject the use of power as the basis for personal relations would also exclude it from international affairs. Some speak as though mutual understanding, trust, and law should be able to replace the use of force in contemporary international affairs. A few historical examples are appropriate here. The historian Herbert Butterfield cited an English bishop who, before World War II, claimed that his high regard for human nature had convinced him that if Great Britain totally disarmed, no other nation would attack it. Though the story of this bishop may have been apocryphal, the 1928 Kellogg-Briand Pact, which sixty-two nations signed to remove war as an instrument of national policy, is a matter of record. So, too, is the famous—or infamous—Oxford resolution of 1933, whose signers agreed that "this House will not fight for King or Country." (It should probably be noted here that many who voted for this resolution served honorably in His Majesty's forces during World War II.) More recently, the members of the Executive Coordinating Committee of the National Council of Churches would have entrusted the United Nations, even in its present state, with the responsibility for maintaining order during the crisis in the Persian Gulf. Part of their resolution of 14 September 1990 "urg[ed] all governments to comply with all resolutions of the United Nations Security Council dealing with the situation in the Middle East."

War and the immediate threat of war understandably draw into the political discussion many who have previously given little thought to the relation between morality and politics, force and national policies. During the Vietnam conflict their numbers multiplied alarmingly. It was alarming because their lack of reflection did not deter them from giving strong advice to those who were responsible for making crucial decisions about national policy. During the 1960s many discovered that the vocabulary of morality had public resonance and could be at least rhetorically useful in discussing political affairs. One well-known Catholic journal said of the war in Vietnam, "It is no longer a political matter, it is now a question of morality."

This sentiment apparently presupposes that ordinary political life can trudge along amorally until, suddenly, it is somehow transmuted into the higher realm of morality—where it can be subjected to different standards of evaluation. An early critic of the war, Bishop Fulton J. Sheen, urged a unilateral withdrawal of American troops, calling this a moral, not a political, response to the war. ("Thanks a lot," says the policymaker.) Religious leaders were especially tempted to react to the messy affair in such a way. It obviated the need for assimilating considerable data and making clear analyses, while it supposedly transmitted a message of deep moral involvement. What those responding in this fashion failed to recognize is that, in political matters, the realm of morality engages the realm of power in actual policy. A "moral" policy that is not simultaneously a political policy is no policy. Moral considerations must pass through the political process before they can inform policy. Acheson's strictures accurately apply to those who fail to acknowledge this fact. Such people supplied the ready moral maxims and slogans to which he objected. They give morality a bad name.

It is at least partially in reaction to such misguided applications of "moral" principles that Acheson, Kennan, and others adopted the positions they did. If morality is what these proponents declared it to be, it is better removed from policy deliberations. It only muddies analyses and confuses decisions. Ironically, in speaking as though they can make substantive moral judgments of policy without mastering the essential political elements, this group forms an unintended alliance with those who believe that they can forge policy without the intrusion of moral principles. The latter group relies entirely on the competence, expertise, and tempered and experienced judgment of the professional. What they fail to realize is that all policy decisions—because they affect the national interests of the United States and, therefore, the welfare of its citizens—inevitably have a moral component. For them this moral component is disguised as a technical matter. Both groups, then, should be judged harshly: both those who would sever morality from politics and those who believe that unmediated moral principles will lead them to appropriate national policies are steeped in intellectual and moral confusion.

Personal and Political Morality Confused

The confusion to which Acheson and his sympathizers direct their justified scorn arises from applying to the entity of the nation-state the standards that apply to a completely different entity, the human person—the "children and friends of God." The differences between the two make it impossible to apply a univocal set of moral standards to both. As Acheson said, these two entities have different ends, different purposes, and different springs of action. Some of the pertinent differences are easily stated:

1. The destiny of the human person is not fully contained within the temporal order—within the confines of earthly history; that of the nation-state is. We are the heirs of eternal glory; the state is not.

2. The moral obligations placed upon the state are narrower than those placed upon the person. Not all sins are crimes, nor can they be.

3. The political ends, the purposes, of the state—I will specify the United States—are of a political order larger than those the person alone can capably address. The preamble to our Constitution lists them concisely: justice, a civil order, security, general welfare, and liberty. Acting collectively, persons in their (strictly limited) political capacity as citizens, can participate in securing these goals. No single person can determine them.

4. The person who discharges political responsibility by assuming the role of statesman or politician will usually specialize in ways that the ordinary citizen will not. Different legislators and advisers, for example, will develop a familiarity with a wide range of specialized knowledge that is not possessed by the average citizen: military technology, legal decisions and judicial precedents, economic determinants, and specific foreign cultures. The average citizen will be unable to advise the experts on the particulars of political decisions that demand that specialized knowledge.

5. The person is able to act for himself directly. The officeholder is an agent who must necessarily act for others. The person can have a private life; the purposes of the state are public. Acting in his nonpolitical role, the individual

affects primarily people he knows personally; he is able to observe and judge the consequences of actions for which he is responsible. The professional politician, and the citizen in his political capacity, must share in a process in which the weight of his considerations is usually difficult to determine.

6. The state has concentrated power at its disposable and a corresponding obligation to use it for proper political ends—those which Kennan enumerated. In this sense, it has a monopoly of legitimate force. The ordinary person does not. The citizen may choose to be a pacifist; the state cannot.

For these and other reasons, the morality proper to personal life cannot be, unequivocally, that of the state. The moral imperatives that inform political action derive from the inherent demands of the political order. When this distinction is not perceived, when Christian standards of personal morality are pressed into service to evaluate and test international policies, one arrives at the tragic—or farcical—confrontation set forth so dramatically but mistakenly by Morgenthau. As president, Jimmy Carter became an exemplar of such confusion. He exhibited both its serious and comedic aspects when he expressed personal outrage that the Soviet ambassador had lied to him—Jimmy Carter. The deeper offense, of course, was that the ambassador had lied to the president of the United States. By personalizing such issues, he failed to distinguish between his ordinary personal goals and responsibilities and those he assumed as the president of the United States.

Foreign Policy and a Moral Compass

If personal moral standards are inappropriate for the demands of the United States in its relations with other countries, is it then destined to set its course on the choppy international waters without a moral compass? Whether it is theoretically possible or desirable for this country to engage other countries without reference to morality, the fact is that the American people will not allow it. Generally tolerant of, and even indifferent to, our foreign policy, the American people will rise to judgment at times of crisis and major political decisions. This is true of such altruistic (or seemingly altruistic) actions as the Marshall Plan, which distributed numerous resources to Western countries after World War II, or to such immoral (or allegedly immoral) actions as the Vietnam War.

On such occasions, the body politic of the United States makes its politico-moral judgment of the policy known and its influence felt—usually to the dismay of some policy-makers. These experts decry the entrance of the public into the arena of international affairs because it interferes with, and sometimes upsets, the carefully made plans that they view as desirable. Such "interference," they assert, muddies the political waters. In response to unwanted public advice, they maintain that such arcane and complicated matters should be decided by experts. Their message is, in effect, "Trust us." Large-scale international policies, however, cannot be sustained over a prolonged period without the broad support of the American people, whose trust is limited. The political actor who does not acknowledge and consider this fact—however much he may bemoan the need to do so—will run unnecessary risks. His great plans may come to naught, and although he may be the president of the United States, he may be removed from office by the citizenry.

What, then, is the moral code suitable to international affairs—the code to which the American people, at least occasionally, refer? Examining some particular cases may better reveal what these principles are than composing an abstract list. In the recent past, nuclear arms and the strategy of nuclear deterrence would certainly have been the first issue to come to mind. The immense scale of the threatened destruction and the immense value of what was at stake made virtually inevitable the use of moral categories in discussions of deterrence. While religious leaders predictably offered moral analyses, even politicos, who normally eschewed "moral talk," found that they needed to draw on a moral vocabulary. Since the collapse of Communism, the international landscape has been considerably altered, and the threat of nuclear war has been consequently reduced. Nevertheless, the threat of, and frequent recourse to, force remain constant factors in international relations and cannot be ignored even if the force is nonnuclear.

Another category of political action that readily inspires "moral talk" and the supposition that our good intentions will direct us unerringly to proper policies is humanitarian aid. What is more self-evident than the idea that those who have much should give to those in dire need—even in international affairs?

Intervention

The two cases I will examine—in Haiti and in Africa—fall under the general rubric of intervention. Intervention, as the term is used here, refers to deliberate actions outside the normal channels of interstate exchange by which one or more states attempts to effect desired changes in the internal affairs of another state. The spectrum of such actions is very wide; it ranges from the use of military force, to economic sanctions, to large-scale humanitarian aid. It includes, paradoxically, the withdrawal or cessation of aid on which the recipient countries have come to rely. It includes threats as well as actions. It may come in opposition to the leadership of the targeted country or at the express invitation of the government of the country. Its ends may be either destructive or benign.

This definition includes, but extends beyond, a common understanding of intervention that limits it to military force. As it relates narrowly to force, the traditional doctrine on which the United States has relied posits that military intervention is justified if it is deemed necessary to defend vital security interests of this country. The threat to those interests need not be military. Intervention is also justified if it is seen as a response to a prior and unjustified intervention by other states. These are the grounds, amply developed, on which the United States relied to justify its intervention in El Salvador, Nicaragua, Grenada, Afghanistan, and the Gulf states.

This traditional doctrine was extended—in ways that are pertinent to our concerns—by President Ronald Reagan. In his State of the Union message in 1985, the president said that "support for freedom fighters is self-defense and totally consistent with the OAS and U.N. charters." He mentioned as "our brothers" in revolution those fighting "in Afghanistan, in Ethiopia, Cambodia, Angola . . . [and] Nicaragua." To these declarations, Secretary of State George P. Shultz added, "America . . . has a moral responsibility. The lesson of the postwar era is that America must be the leader of the free world; there is no one else to take our place."

The exact dimensions of the Reagan Doctrine, as it came to be called, have been much debated. One notable defender of the doctrine, Charles Krauthammer, has said that it "proclaims overt and unashamed American support for anti-Communist revolution. The grounds are justice, necessity, and democratic tradition." There is little doubt that President Reagan had Communist governments in mind when he enunciated his doctrine, but it was expressed in universalist terms. The justification for overthrowing Communist governments was that they were illegitimate—morally illegitimate because they were not based on democratic processes and were neither empowered by nor responsive to their people.

Although the number of Communist governments has now greatly diminished, the principle of the Reagan Doctrine remains—and remains to be applied to non-Communist governments. For if the sovereignty of a Communist state can be breached morally, why not the sovereignty of an admittedly foul non-Communist regime? "How awful must a government be," Krauthammer asks, "before it fails the moral protection of sovereignty and before justice permits its violent removal? . . . By what logic should support be denied to those fighting indigenous tyranny?"[6]

Such questions are asked by people who would invoke the Reagan Doctrine when they contemplate possible options presented by the current "democratic revolution." If the United States, they argue, can support, at relatively low cost, indigenous movements that are attempting to replace harsh, unjust regimes with democracies—however fragile—is it not desirable to help them?

Few would oppose the extension of freedoms to those who do not have them or the securing of freedoms against internal attacks, but whether the United States should intervene to ensure the desirable outcome—and at what cost—is difficult to answer in the abstract. That issue raises all the questions posed by traditional teachings on just war. Before taking any action, we would have to estimate as closely as possible the cost to the United States, to the people of the country being helped, and to the international order within which this interstate action takes place. Will this particular action, for example, enhance or erode the possibilities of nonviolent conflict resolution between states? Will it weaken or strengthen possibilities of international cooperation between states?

Haiti

In its efforts to establish a viable, democratic government, Haiti presents a case in point. Haiti, which occupies the western third of a Caribbean island and has a population of 6.5 million people, has had an almost unbroken history of poverty, violence, and oppressive regimes since it achieved independence in 1804 as the world's first black republic. In 1986 a military coup ended almost thirty years of dictatorial rule by the Duvalier family. A rapid succession of rulers followed in the next few years, which were marked by bloody repression of human-rights activists and dissenting politicians. This period of turmoil led to an agreement to have internationally monitored elections in December 1990.

In a process that was judged to be fair and free, the Haitian people chose a president, a bicameral parliament, and municipal officials. The elected president was the Rev. Jean-Bernard Aristide, a young, charismatic, socialist, Catholic priest. The new president had to deal with a military that regarded itself as almost autonomous and was ready to impose civil "order"; the dreaded Tontons Macoute, who marauded at will under the Duvaliers to whom alone they were loyal and subservient; a very weak judicial system; skeptical foreign diplomats; Haitian businessmen and foreign investors who were apprehensive because of his socialist rhetoric; a local Church hierarchy that had tried to have him expelled; a depressed economy; and the many poor peasants who had supported him and were impatient for improvements in their status and living conditions.

Despite—or because of—these conditions, early economic aid was offered by the United States, France, and other developed countries, and was gratefully received by Aristide. The early months of Aristide's rule brought mixed, but generally favorable, reviews from observers, including spokesmen for U.S. policy. Aristide's rhetoric had been toned down; he sought to heal the breach between himself and the Church hierarchy; he continued his assault on the Tontons Macoute; and he encouraged the establishment of justice under law. In a country whose political culture knew little of democratic law and civil order, he was called upon to develop it.

On 30 September 1990, soon after he had returned from a

visit to the United States and to the United Nations, Aristide was unseated in a military coup and forced to flee his country. The coup was accompanied by protests, a bloody crackdown, and a militarily imposed parliamentary ruling that provided a provisional president. Those who led the coup and some of Haiti's elite were pleased to see Aristide overthrown, and some of his political opponents said that he had brought it upon himself. The larger body of Haitians continued their support for the exiled president.

Spokesmen for the U.S. government immediately backed Aristide, called for his return as the duly elected president, and promised to work within the charter of the Organization of American States to effect his return. Speaking to an ad hoc meeting of OAS ministers of foreign affairs on 2 October 1991, the representative from Grenada recalled an earlier statement delivered by his country:

> Whereas the electoral process determines who governs, the management of the system between elections indicates the extent to which the democratic culture is evolving. The democratic culture definitely promotes respect for the observance of human rights and tolerance for alternative viewpoints. In short, the democratic culture, in the heart and consciousness of the people is the best insurance against the arbitrary exercise of power or the subversion of constitutional order.

He then added, "Whereas the internal affairs of a country are its own business, the large-scale violation of human rights is a crime against humanity which would necessitate strong international action."

The following day, the OAS ministers approved by unanimous vote a resolution that included a demand for the immediate reinstatement of President Jean-Bernard Aristide. Amid these and other strong calls for the return of Aristide and support for democracy, an unsettling note intruded. Although

Aristide had come into office advising his followers to forego vengeance, it was reported that, upon his return from his warm reception at the United Nations, he had addressed the Haitian people in an exhortation that sounded to some like an incitement to further lawless violence. While granting that he had been democratically elected and was still supported by a vast majority of the Haitian people, policy-makers had to decide whether Aristide was the kind of person they wanted to restore to his presidency by a show of force.

Because the OAS was acting within accepted international law, the United States as a member of the organization did not need to invoke the Reagan Doctrine. Nevertheless, those U.S. officials responsible for our reaction to this ongoing situation had to depend on reasoning similar to that underlying the Reagan Doctrine. They had to consider the baleful effects of an embargo on the populace of a poor country that depends on imports for most of its food stuffs; the position of Aristide if he were returned to power under OAS pressures, and the strengthened position of the Haitian military if he were not; the effect of their decisions on the rule of international law if the OAS took a strong, active position; whether the nascent democratic culture that was emerging in Haiti could be both restored and strengthened; and whether the attempt to restore it was compatible with possibly continuing human-rights abuses. There were other serious considerations, but these few indicate how many variables are involved in the decision-making process. Where are the principles that guide those who are called upon to make such decisions?

Humanitarian Aid

Putting aside, temporarily, even tentative answers to such questions, let us turn to a form of intervention that, at least initially, would seem to pose no such problems—the supply of emergency food aid to countries with hungry or starving populations. The United States regularly produces surplus food. Various countries around the world suffer, at least sporadically, from drought, flooding, blight, and unsuccessful agricultural experiments. The moral equation seems beyond dispute. The United States, either alone or with other agencies, should distribute food to the needy countries.

Our experience in attempting to do so, however, has not been uniformly happy. Many of the results have been not only unexpected but counterintuitive and counterproductive. In 1984, five million African children died from hunger-related causes.[7] In the mid-1980s, approximately one-third of the Africans who lived below the Sahara needed emergency food. This occurred *after* two decades of food-aid programs. Here were some of their unexpected results:

—Some projects that had worked well elsewhere, such as deep plowing, chemical fertilizers, the Green Revolution, did not transplant to Africa. In some areas an acre of land was lost to farming for every one that was successfully developed.

—In some areas, rice production fell by one-third because the imported rice seed had low resistance to Africa's environment and did not do well.

—During the 1970s the West contributed over $22 billion in economic-development aid to sub-Saharan Africa. In the 1970s, the per capita food production fell by approximately 1.2 per cent a year. (Some of the projects that were funded by this money, and that proved ineffective at best, were urged on the African countries by the donor nations.)

—Long-term food aid, according to one analyst, "may depress farm prices in the aid area, not reach those who need food most, promote shifts in food-consumption patterns away from local foods to imported foods, encourage dependence on make-work and food handouts, and . . . reduce the incentive of recipient African nations to develop and carry out agricultural-policy reforms."

—The prime beneficiaries of food aid sometimes proved to be, not those for whom it was intended, but wealthy farmers and food-aid bureaucracies.

—Food aid undermined the price structure of locally produced food, sometimes overwhelming already marginalized farmers.

—Some farmers who received aid in one year reduced the amount of sown grain the following year, because they expected similar aid once again. The effect was to lower local production and necessitate higher imports of food.

—Even when the need for short-term food aid subsides, the distribution of food continues. The complicated distribution system remains in place, along with the administrators who run it. It has developed a momentum of its own. The result is to exacerbate a situation that the system was intended to alleviate.

It is true that some valuable lessons have been learned from the many years of failures and successes. In the future, both donors and their African recipients may be able to avoid some pitfalls and capitalize on the successes. And one important lesson stands out among all the others: the problem is much more complicated than it seems; ample resources, dedicated people, and good intentions often prove inadequate to the reality. The tragic predicament in Somalia shows just how tangled such situations can become.

Reality and Perceived Reality

One last bit of evidence attests to the uncertainty in which policy-makers must make large-scale decisions. While one presumes that the CIA has more intelligence available than do individuals or most other governmental agencies, Robert M. Gates's testimony before the Senate Select Committee on Intelligence as they considered his nomination to be director of the agency is telling:

While our list of successes is impressive, the list of our shortcomings, the events where we fell short, is in some ways even more impressive. We failed adequately to predict the scope of Soviet strategic deployments during the late 1960s and early 1970s. We failed to anticipate technological breakthroughs such as those that led to the deployment of the Alpha-class submarine. We missed the revolution in Iran. We failed to predict the Soviet invasion of Afghanistan until they actually began their military preparations. We failed over a number of years to identify for our policy-makers the magnitude of Soviet efforts to acquire Western technology, and the nature of those efforts. We failed to anticipate the Egyptian decision to launch a war against Israel in 1973. We significantly misjudged the percentage of Soviet G.N.P. allocated to defense. We have repeatedly misread Cuba. We ignored Soviet interest in terrorism. We have been far behind events in devoting resources to examining instability and insurgency, and that is not an exhaustive list.

I think that among the failures would be most recently the failure to anticipate Saddam Hussein's invasion of Kuwait. It would be the Soviet recognition that they could no longer sustain the level of defense spending that they had with the economic troubles that they had.[8]

All the different examples that have now been cited—Haiti, humanitarian aid, intelligence (or the lack of it)—point to undeniable home truths: large-scale decisions on the international plane depend on much information, which is not always available. When available, the information must be evaluated in the light of other strategic-political possibilities. The decision that appears to promise the optimal outcome for the United States may not do so. In numerous instances, the measures taken intensify the conditions that they were designed to cure. Even when coupled with the fullest available information and the highest expertise that our country can offer, good intentions and high moral principles are often insufficient.

Political Responsibilities—A Hierarchical Order

At this point, it seems appropriate to return to early concerns—to recall the general framework, which stresses the infirmity of humankind, its weaknesses, and the flaws that run through all of its faculties. While acknowledging that much difficult and uncertain terrain must be traversed before policy decisions are made, we know that such decisions must be made. And here, a necessary division of responsibility occurs. In the United States, indeed, we have elected and appointed representatives to conduct affairs of state, including foreign affairs. They have the responsibility to act in our collective interest to ensure, in the words of the preamble to the Constitution, our security and well-being. Although George Kennan would not agree, that is both a political and a moral responsibility.

Other citizens have obligations according to their own positions in our society. Political analysts and advisers, businessmen, religious leaders, academics, journalists, and average citizens will operate differently and will have varying degrees of influence. But the first duty of the American statesman is to recognize clearly the interests of the United States without disregarding or blinding himself to those of other countries. The interests of the United States will be defined concretely by a series of particular decisions and definite actions in which immediate concerns play only a small part. Every decision will be made in a developing tradition of what constitutes our national interest. Drawing upon the political culture of our society, this tradition will provide broad guidelines rather than a blueprint. Within those broad guidelines, the statesman must make the particular decisions that will form our foreign policy.

Now we come to a crux in our examination of ethical reasoning in political decisions. The best decisions will be dictated by prudence, which is easily said but not easily formulated for timely consumption. The virtue of prudence must be distinguished from its colloquial definition. It is not a synonym for caution, wiliness, timidity, moderation, or George Bush. Using the term within the context of international affairs, the great political theorist Raymond Aron wrote:

> To be prudent is to act in accordance with the particular situation and the concrete data, and not in accordance with some system, or out of passive obedience to a norm or pseudo-norm; it is to prefer the limitation of violence to the punishment of the presumably guilty party or to a so-called absolute justice; it is to establish concrete accessible objectives conforming to the secular law of international relations and not to limitless and perhaps meaningless objectives, such as "a world safe for democracy" or "a world from which power politics will have disappeared."[9]

In his small book on prudence, the distinguished philosopher Joseph Pieper explores more fully the rich and profound meaning that should attach to this word. Prudence is, he states, the cause, root, measure, and guide of all ethical virtues. Only the prudent can truly be just, brave, or temperate. At the risk of seriously diminishing Pieper's exploration, I extract two observations applicable to our concerns:

—The imperative of prudence is always and in essence a decision regarding an action to be performed in the "here and now." By their very nature such decisions can be made only by the person confronted with decision.

—The content of a prudent decision is, rather, determined by the *ipsa res*, by reality, which is the "measure" of all cognition and decision. Desiring the good does not make a decision prudent; but real understanding and proper evaluation of the concrete situation of the concrete act does.[10]

The overlap is evident between Aron's statement, which is expressly directed to international affairs, and Pieper's exploration, which is intended to recall and revive classical Christian understanding of the virtue of prudence. Both stress the need to perceive the situation as well as the necessary data.

This understanding of the statesman's role does not reduce the role of other citizens to a nullity. Each individual, in his respective capacity, is called upon to act prudently if he is to make fully ethical decisions—including decisions made in his political role as a citizen. Individuals address the political issues that demand political resolution in different ways and, again according to their respective responsibilities and capacities, transmit their best decisions to the lawmakers. In this way, each person becomes a part of the situation—a part of the concrete reality—that the policy-maker must consider. He will be most imprudent if he does not.

This advisory function is complemented by a necessarily reactive function. If the policy-maker eventually makes numerous decisions that, in the light of their results, citizens judge to be poor or even harmful, they can call for a reassessment of the policy-maker and his policies. This call for reassessment can occur gradually in the regular course of the political process, or it can manifest itself in demonstrations such as those that accompanied the civil-rights and antiwar movements of the 1960s. In this way, the democratic process allows the body politic to place constraints that are simultaneously political and moral on U.S. policies. The value of the advice that the body politic offers to, and of the constraints that it imposes on, the decision-making process will be directly proportional to the political prudence of the body politic.

The right to offer advice and impose constraints, then, is

accompanied by the possibility of being judged. The person or group that regularly advances advice that, in retrospect, appears to have been prudent will gain credibility and respect—and greater influence. Imprudent advice, on the other hand, will eventually erode its proponents' credibility and respect. The National Council of Churches seems to have an inexhaustible supply of political advice to offer to U.S. policymakers, for example, but its currency rings ever more hollow. Judgment runs on a two-way street in these matters.

Morality and "Morality"

These foregoing reflections constitute a response—and a partial refutation—to those who argue as Acheson did. But something more remains to be said. There is a common confusion, which is partly semantic and partly real, about the relationship between morality and politics. Acheson contributed to this confusion, which some extreme examples will help to highlight.

First, there is a frequent tendency to limit the concept of morality so that judgments may be presented as value-free and nonmoralistic. The editorials, subheads, and news stories of the *New York Times* provide a wealth of examples:

—"It is not a matter of morality, it's a matter of a woman's right to choose."

—The city's distribution of condoms in high schools "is not a question of morality, it's a question of life and death."

—"This is not a matter of morality, it is a matter of personal integrity."

Such confusion about what constitutes morality seems too blatant to require comment. (If matters of life and death are not matters of morality, one wonders, what might be?) Another example comes to mind. Musing on the Vietnam War after it ended, Eugene McCarthy, who was known to be something of a moralist, said that he did not oppose the war on political or moral grounds. He said that he simply came to believe that it was costing too much in lives and resources for what it was worth. Surprisingly, he did not seem to realize that he was invoking the principle of proportionality, which is clearly a moral criterion established by the "just war" tradition to assess the justice of wars.

In deciding whether to intervene in Haiti or in other shaky democracies, to attempt to contain violence in the former Yugoslavia, to give large-scale aid to African countries or to the republics of what was until recently the Soviet Union, or to be confrontational in bilateral talks on the trade policies of Japan, policy-makers will be making judgments that are simultaneously political and moral. It cannot be otherwise. Their decisions will affect the lives of Americans, and many others, and they will necessarily reflect the values of the American people.

Those high officials who will shape policy issues may take this so much for granted that they fail to realize they are operating on presuppositions that are part of our political culture. If they chose to express their own views and were as articulate as Dean Acheson or George Kennan, they would probably sound very much like them. After listening to a presentation similar to my own, a typical high-level official responded in bemused and ironic tones, "Well, I didn't realize all these years that I was making moral judgments. I thought I was just doing what I was trained for, saying yes here and no there and so on." He and others like him remind me of Molière's ladies who spoke prose for years without knowing it. And, just as it did not matter that the ladies were unaware they were speaking prose as along as they did it well, it does not matter greatly that policy-makers do not realize they are making moral judgments as long as they make them prudently. It is, after all, better to be prudent than to be able to discuss the virtue learnedly.

At this point, we have returned to the concepts that provided the framework within which the rest of the discussion is contained. We have returned, that is, to the explicit recognition that we are all children of God, that we are united in our common humanity, that we are graced with equal dignity, and that this deep recognition should inform our actions in the political realm. To do this effectively, we must adhere in our culture, most particularly our political culture, to the values we hold most deeply as the children of God.

Response

Richard D. Land

I would certainly agree with James Finn that Dean Acheson's formulation leaves us wide of the mark. Acheson, Hans Morgenthau, Henry Kissinger, and many in the Bush—and no doubt in the Clinton—administration seem to know in great detail the price of almost everything and the value of relatively few things. Indeed, they seem not to know, or to think irrelevant, the value of some very important things. But for those of us who do believe that there are moral constraints and responsibilities, the question is how far do those constraints and responsibilities take us? We are all creatures of God, but only those who have entered into a personal relationship with him would be considered his children. Therein lies the enormous difference between the City of God and the City of Man.

When he spoke of a moral man in an immoral society, Reinhold Niebuhr was not denying the sinfulness of individuals. He was insisting only that we could demand a higher standard of fallen men individually than we could demand of fallen man collectively. We did, however, have to demand standards of both. The great commandment of Christian ethics is not "love thy neighbor as thyself"; it is "love the Lord thy God with all thy heart, with all thy mind, with all

---

Richard D. Land is the executive director of the Christian Life Commission of the Southern Baptist Convention.

thy soul." Loving our neighbor is one way of loving God. Ethical difficulties arise when we try to separate the two because they cannot be separated. We cannot know what it means to love our neighbors without first seeking God and his righteousness.

The "mustard plaster approach" Finn criticizes does present problems, but so does an entirely flexible approach. I think there is something very attractive in Jimmy Carter's designation of himself as "first servant"—in the idea that public service is a service and that politics is not a means to itself but a means to an end. For those of us who come from a Christian tradition, it is a moral means to moral ends. We forget that to our peril.

When I read the statement, "The confusion . . . arises from applying to the entity of the nation-state the standards that apply to a completely different entity, the human person," I become concerned. I disagree with that. There *is* a single, absolute moral standard. Truth is truth. It is true personally; it is true collectively; it is true universally. It is always true. We do not need to have different standards, but, rather, to apply the same basic standards intelligently, adjusting for different circumstances.

Before the Gulf War, James Baker and George Bush seemed perplexed and mystified that Americans were not eager to go to war for oil or jobs. The kind of intervention they advocated in the Middle East did not gain wide support until they began to speak of resisting aggression, of bringing about a more just and equitable peace and security for the region. In other words, only when they talked in terms that had moral resonance with the American people were their plans accepted.

We are not, and have never been, a nation in the ordinary sense of the word. We are in many ways unique. This does not mean that the United States is God's chosen nation or the successor of Israel. It does not mean that God has a special relationship with the American people. It does mean, however, that our nation still has the heart and soul of our Puritan ancestors and still sees itself as "a city on the hill." America has in many ways been, and remains, a cause. It is a group of people held together by allegiance to a common set of ideas and ideals. And prudence is not one of the ideals that would leap to mind.

Large-scale international policies cannot be sustained over a prolonged period of time without the broad support of the American people. Ronald Reagan's extension of the doctrine of intervention was probably not very prudent. He was, in fact, criticized for not being prudent, for being too ideological or "value-laden" in matters of foreign policy. But it was precisely because he was not prudent that he broke the back of the Soviet empire.

Part of prudence is to see reality clearly, and we should certainly try to assess each situation as realistically as possible. We must not, however, be dictated to by reality. There are times when reality must be overridden by conviction and by an absolute moral standard, even if that means making considerable sacrifices or risking our very existence, individually or collectively. But such decisions cannot—and should not—be made by our leaders unilaterally. At best we should aspire to elect to office the kind of men and women who will come to us with the facts and say, "This is something I believe we should do. We may not be able to pull it off, it may cost us, we may fail, we may be defeated, but I believe there is nothing else we can do. If the American people then say they support that course of action, it becomes acceptable.

We fool ourselves if we think that any discussions, decisions, or policies are made in a moral vacuum. Belief in that myth is limited to certain twentieth-century American secularists. All decisions come from a moral presuppositional base. The only question is what the operative morals and presuppostions are.

When presidential candidate John F. Kennedy met with Baptist ministers in Houston and vowed that his Catholicism would have very little to do with his service as president, that he was an American first and a Catholic second, it should have caused many to pause. Would we want to elect someone who denies that his faith would influence his conduct in office?

Strict adherence to the virtue of prudence might well have robbed human history of some of its finest hours. Was it prudent for Winston Churchill, almost by force of his will alone, to keep the British Empire in the war against Germany after the fall of France? Because of some absolute moral convictions about the evil he faced, he was willing to risk the very survival of Great Britain and its empire to stand against what he considered a monstrous evil. Would it have been considered prudent in the late spring of 1776 for our forefathers to declare their independence from Britain? Was it prudent for Harry Truman to recognize, unequivocally and absolutely, the state of Israel on May 1, 1948? Would it have been the prudent thing to do, had we all had the facts, to vote for Abraham Lincoln in the late fall of 1860?

Imprudent actions, then, *can* produce excellent results, and prudent actions, despicable ones. The United States was no doubt prudent when it decided not to intervene on the side of the Hungarians in 1956. It was prudent when it accepted the Berlin Wall in 1963. But if Ronald Reagan had been president in those years, he might very well have both intervened on the side of the Hungarians and knocked down the Wall. He might have revealed the bluster and hollowness of the Soviet empire and caused its collapse thirty years earlier. It would not have been prudent, but a lot of people would have been saved a lot of misery. And it would have been right.

3

The Poverty of
Conventional Realism

George Weigel

With the death of Communism and the waning of the Cold War, a three-sided strategic and moral debate over the future course of U.S. foreign policy quickly emerged. The anti-Communist coalition that won the "long, twilight struggle" splintered; erstwhile colleagues in the formulation and execution of the Reagan Doctrine found themselves at cross-purposes. Traditional isolationism, long associated with the Old Right, was resuscitated through a Hatfields-and-McCoys wedding to the neo-isolationism of the Vietnam-era New Left. And as if that were not enough, a new argument erupted about the viability of realism (in either its classic European/ *realpolitik* form or its modern American/Niebuhrian construal) as a guide for American action in the world. The parallels to the 1930s are unmistakable: "back to the future" may well define the foreign-policy debate in the 1990s.

Perhaps the most curious of these related phenomena has

George Weigel is the president of the Ethics and Public Policy Center and the author or editor of twelve books, including *The Final Revolution: The Resistance Church and the Collapse of Communism*.

been the isolationist renaissance. Once regarded as having been consigned to the murkier nether regions of our public discourse, isolationism (or, as its exponents prefer, the new nationalism or "noninterventionism") has once again become a significant voice in the argument over the national interest and the national purpose. (It may seem passing strange that people who drive Hondas, shave with Braun razors, watch Sony TVs, prepare their pesto sauce in Cuisinarts, sip Perrier, Corona, and Glenfiddich, and listen to Deutsche Grammophon recordings should be susceptible to the siren songs of autarky; but, as the metaphysician Yogi Berra is supposed to have said when a Jew was elected mayor of Dublin, "only in America.") Indeed, it is entirely possible that the 1996 presidential election will be fought in part on ground defined by the renewal of the old McGovernite call to "Come home, America."

The political potency of the new isolationism has been made possible in large part by the puzzling rapprochement between two hitherto antithetical perceptions of the United States and its role in world affairs. Old Right isolationism, of the sort championed during the 1941 Lend Lease debate by figures like Senators Gerald Nye of North Dakota and Burton K. Wheeler of Montana, taught U.S. withdrawal from the raw world of European politics because engagement with morally malodorous foreigners would inevitably sully the American experiment in democratic republicanism. They were corrupt; we were pure; we should stay out. The neo-isolationism of the New Left during the Vietnam period inverted this analysis. America should "come home" because a racist, imperialist, militarist (and, latterly, sexist) United States would corrupt the emerging nations of the Third World. We were corrupt; they were pure; we should get out.

The debate over U.S. policy after Saddam Hussein's invasion and occupation of Kuwait in August 1990 brought to the surface the truce that had been arranged between these antinomies, now reconciled (if only tactically) by their common aversion to "interventionism" and President Bush's "New World Order." During the argument over whether Desert Shield should give way to Desert Storm, one wag (a Quaker activist, actually) had campaign buttons printed up that read: "McGovern/Buchanan: The PEACE ticket for '92." In view of Patrick J. Buchanan's forthright embrace of "America First" as a theme in his subsequent campaign and the announcement speeches of several Democratic presidential aspirants in the fall of 1991, other buttons reading "Harkin/Buchanan" or "Kerrey/Buchanan" or "Gephardt/Buchanan" would have captured this sensibility just as nicely.

This bizarre symbiosis has acquired more intellectual credibility than it might otherwise enjoy because the visceral isolationism of the Old Right/New Left activists has been tempered, and the "new nationalist" prescription amplified, by the emergence of libertarian scholars and publicists such as Ted Galen Carpenter and Doug Bandow of the Cato Institute, and harder-to-classify analysts like Alan Tonelson of the Economic Policy Institute, all of whom have pressed the new isolationism vigorously (and without the xenophobia so sadly characteristic of some of Buchanan's writing). It was, in fact, a potent sign of the times that the work of Carpenter, the Cato libertarian isolationist, should be prominently displayed in *Foreign Policy*, originally founded as the establishmentarian vehicle for the propagation of the Vietnam-era neo-isolationist creed. Whatever its ideological wellsprings, though, isolationism is back; and considering its resonance with deep-running currents in the national culture and psyche, to ignore it is preemptively to concede the argument to it.

Opposing the New Isolationism

The most visible challenge to the new isolationism in the immediate aftermath of the Cold War was mounted by a cadre of academics and commentators who might be styled the "democratic internationalists." This cluster of opinion, which emphasized the inescapable necessity of American leadership in a newly unipolar world, and which stressed the possibility of that leadership's effectively creating the conditions for peace with freedom and security through the defense and advancement of democracy, included representatives from chastened liberalism (Joseph S. Nye, Jr., of the Kennedy School at Harvard), neo-conservatism (the columnist Charles Krauthammer and Joshua Muravchik of the American Enterprise Institute), and the Kemp wing of the Republican Party (Gregory Fossedal of the Hoover Institution).

The democratic internationalists insisted that theirs is an analysis shorn of the moralistic illusions often associated (rightly or wrongly) with Woodrow Wilson and (quite rightly) with Franklin D. Roosevelt. And indeed, the democratic internationalists tended to be far more skeptical of international organizations and institutions than the liberal internationalists of the interwar and postwar periods. In the post–Cold War, unipolar world of the 1990s and beyond, the democratic internationalists argued, the alternative to American leadership was not multipolarity but chaos.

Moreover, the democratic internationalists insisted that the Reagan Doctrine—of vigorous support for democratic forces, be they in Chile, Afghanistan, or Poland—was not simply an interim or emergency measure whose rationale was provided by its repulsive mirror image, the Brezhnev Doctrine. Rather, democratic internationalists saw the post–Cold War task of the United States—defending democratic allies and resisting aggression by crazy states where necessary, promoting democratic transitions where possible, and supporting democratic consolidation in countries formerly run by commissars or caudillos—as emerging from the very nature of the United States itself (a country founded on certain claims about the inalienable rights of the human person), from America's successful leadership of the Party of Freedom in World War III (the Cold War), and from a prudent calculation of the national interest.

Then there were the realists. The democratic internationalists claimed to have learned from the critique of Wilsonian idealism mounted by the realist school of the 1930s and 1940s, but several prominent commentators who self-consciously identify with that critique disagreed. Irving Kristol, Owen Harries, Robert W. Tucker (all of *National Interest*), Jeane J. Kirkpatrick, and Henry Kissinger did not agree on everything (neither, for that matter, did Krauthammer and Nye, much less Harkin and Buchanan). But they did seem at one in thinking that the democratic-internationalist proposal was too optimistic in its reading of the possibilities at the end of the twentieth century, too sanguine about the relationship between democracy and international cooperation, and too little attentive to the fundamental conflicts that still define the fault lines in international public life today.

The realist counter-proposal, for a return to "normalcy" in the conduct of our foreign policy, was built around the concept of "the national interest," which was defined in political-military and economic terms. The realists were not, and are not, autarkists. While they cringed at the word "interdependence," they understood the facts of modern international economic life, and they took seriously the claim that the Great Depression was caused at least in part by the tariff wars of the 1920s. The realists were not, in other words, isolationists with a big stick and an aggressive exports policy.

On the other hand, the realists denied that defining the national interest involved calculations beyond the strictly political-military and economic. They stressed the limits of American power and the inevitability of chaos and unpredictability in world politics. They understood that "intractable" is a sad but accurate description of the nature of certain conflicts (such as the Middle East). And they had grave doubts about the willingness of the American people to support (and pay for) a democratic internationalism whose immediate benefits to the United States, particularly in an era of domestic austerity, collapsing infrastructure, and massive trade imbalances, were not immediately evident.

The Triumph of Realism

In the world of ideas, the outcome of this triangular debate among the isolationists, the democratic internationalists, and the realists remained undecided, but in the world of policy, realism won. Indeed, at the higher altitudes of the Bush administration, a particularly constrained, even wizened form of realism quietly emerged as a strategic frame of reference. For George Bush and his people, the New World Order was not to be understood, in even a chastened or tough-minded way, on Wilsonian terms—that is, as a matter of American leadership in the construction of an international political community. Rather, Bush's New World Order resembled nothing so much as the Concert of Europe between, roughly, the Congress of Vienna (1815) and the Franco-Prussian War (1870).

In this respect, Bush administration realism was far more akin to classic European *realpolitik* than it was to the realism of, say, Reinhold Niebuhr or even Dean Acheson, both of whom were deeply influenced by biblical concepts of the inherent irony, pathos, and tragedy of the human condition, and by Augustine's seminal distinction between the City of God and the earthly city. So it is probably a good idea, even in the aftermath of the Bush administration, to distinguish this approach—call it "conventional realism"—from the more richly textured realism of Niebuhr and Acheson and their contemporary heirs such as Kissinger, Kristol, Harries, and Kirkpatrick.

Conventional realism *à la* Bush had several defining characteristics. It seemed, first, quite leery about committing the United States to the pursuit of any great principle in the conduct of our foreign policy. Indeed, one of the striking things about President Bush's repeated call for a New World Order was the lack of content in the operative word, "order" (the same was true for the president's pursuit of "peace"). Thus it should have come as no surprise that, in his September 1991 address to the United Nations General Assembly, less than a month after the New Russian Revolution, Bush carefully avoided rhetoric that could be construed as endorsing the claim that the events of recent years had been an unprecedented triumph for Western conceptions of human rights and a dramatic confirmation of the superiority of democracy as a political system. (Perhaps the thought of the Saudi president of the General Assembly made the White House speechwriters even more circumspect than usual.) The president did say soothing (and unexceptionable) things about free markets and free polities. But there was no ideological or moral passion evident in his rather flaccid address.

The Reagan Doctrine, which was about the struggle between ideas and values as much as it was about the clash of interests, seemed as dead in the Bush administration as it would have been under Michael Dukakis. Indeed, the Bush men seemed at times to go out of their way to distinguish their "pragmatic" approach to the world from the more "ideological" style of the previous administration. And while there may well be something to be said for the realist critique of general moral principles as tactical policy guides (given the endless complexities and imponderabilities of world politics), the failure to articulate the meaning of such terms as "peace" and "order"—and thereby to lend some guiding shape to the definition and execution of policy—tended to yield an American approach to the world reminiscent of Winston Churchill's famous description of a disappointing dessert: "This pudding lacks a theme."

Then there was the president's much-remarked fondness for personal diplomacy. Realism had always been skeptical of popular and congressional involvement in the foreign-policy process (and, on the evidence supplied by Congress over the past twenty years, not without reason). But Bush seemed to have sharpened this aspect of realism to an especially fine point, not least in his successful and admirable creation of the broad coalition that challenged Saddam Hussein and ejected him from Kuwait. Conversely, however, the strength of the president's personal diplomacy under certain circumstances was not infrequently transformed into a weakness when circumstances changed. The emir of Kuwait and the Saudi royal family were far more cooperative before February 28, 1991, than they were afterwards. That was, perhaps, to have been expected. But can we not wonder whether the personalization of the relationship between President Bush and these allies made it more difficult than necessary to keep them on board when the issue became winning the peace rather than winning the war?

Stability Above All

Insofar as it had a guiding concept, the Bush administration's instinctive passion seemed to be for "stability." Here, the president and his foreign-policy advisers most resembled the statesmen at the Congress of Vienna. Like Metternich, Castlereagh, and Talleyrand, President Bush, Secretary of State James A. Baker, and National Security Adviser Brent Scowcroft were men made profoundly uncomfortable by revolutionary ideas and indeed by revolutionaries—and yet they were responsible for U.S. foreign policy in an age of revolution. Here, the issue of personalization intersected with the Bush administration's insistence on stability: confronted with the choice between reform Communist and centralizer Mikhail Gorbachev, on the one hand, and radical democrat and decentralizer Boris Yeltsin, on the other, the Bush administration unhesitatingly chose Gorbachev. (Even more oddly, but just as predictably, the president and his men got around to recognizing the Baltic republics, whose independence the United States had asserted for fifty years, only after Iceland and Denmark.)

Perhaps the best way to sum up the conventional realism of the Bush administration is to say that it was a realism profoundly skeptical of ideology and its role in the affairs of men and nations. This seemed curious (as the realist Owen Harries has himself noted) in the age of Lenin, Hitler, Mao, and Pol Pot; of Gandhi and the Fabian professoriate at the London School of Economics in the 1930s; of Churchill and the founders of the state of Israel; and, more recently, of Havel, Michnik, and Wojtyla. That ideas have consequences is a cliché whose truth has been proven beyond cavil over the past century, and not least in international affairs. But it is a truth that seemed not to have much impressed itself upon the minds and hearts of the conventional realists of the Bush administration.

This profound skepticism about ideology—and particularly the ideology of "democratization" and its roots in the Reagan Doctrine—seems the best explanation for the administration's actions (or inactions) at four defining moments during its stewardship of U.S. foreign policy.

Tiananmen Square

Critics of the Bush administration's response to the shooting of nonviolent, pro-democracy Chinese dissidents in Peking's Tiananmen Square in June 1989 have sometimes suggested that the administration had within its power the capacity to bring down the regime of Deng Xiaoping and thus to usher in a democratic era in China. Yet what one sensed at the time now seems even clearer in retrospect: China had not yet developed that critical mass of "civil society" that made the Revolution of 1989 in Central and Eastern Europe and the New Russian Revolution of August 1991 possible.

That being said, however, the administration's response to the Dengist repression was distressingly tepid, and illustrated the perils of both a self-consciously amoral or *realpolitik* policy calculus (our interests could be best pursued with the repressors) and the personalization of diplomacy (the president and Deng were old friends). The Bush administration could have, and ought to have, declared its support, and even enthusiasm, for the goals of the student dissidents and their nonviolent methods; they were, after all, modeling their revolution explicitly on ours, and the icon they erected in the square, the "Goddess of Democracy," was deliberately evocative of a familiar statue in New York harbor.

What would such a declaration by Bush have accomplished? It might have provided a minimum of protection to the students by signaling Deng and his gerontocratic comrades that they would pay a steep price for repression. It might have strengthened the hand of reformist forces (and they do exist) within the Chinese Communist party—precisely the party forces we ought to encourage in the run-up to post-Deng China. It might have positioned the United States for a brokerage role in the scramble for power—which could well involve massive civil unrest—that will follow Deng's departure for the bosom of Lenin. It might, in other words, have created conditions for the possibility of American leadership in assisting the process of de-Stalinization in China.

Instead, by its emphasis on stability and order, and by its subsequent insistence on maintaining most-favored-nation trading status for the Dengist People's Republic of China, the Bush administration effectively removed the United States from the calculations of the chief actors in the unfolding drama of China. The Dengists did not fear us, and were thus far less likely to change their ways. The reformists did not quite trust us, and thus we will have less leverage with them in the post-Deng power sweepstakes. And the radical democrats felt betrayed. In the name of stability, the Bush administration may have helped create circumstances in which the prospects for an orderly transition beyond Deng have been sadly diminished.

The Endgame in Iraq

President Bush's masterful assembly of the anti-Saddam coalition after the Iraqi invasion and occupation of Kuwait, his firm resistance to the pusillanimity of the Democratic congressional leadership, and the effective conduct of the air and ground wars against Iraq between January 16 and February 28, 1991—none of these accomplishments can, or should, be gainsaid. What was troubling, however, and precisely in terms of parsing the administration's conventional realism, was what happened before August 2, 1990, and after February 28, 1991.

Prior to the Iraqi invasion of Kuwait, Bush administration policy seemed bent on engaging Saddam Hussein as a potential ally in the pursuit of a comprehensive Middle East peace settlement. Counsels to the contrary—counsels that stressed the nature of the Iraqi Baathist regime and the pathologies of Saddam himself—were ignored, presumably on the grounds that Saddam was the major Arab military power in the region and thus had to be dealt with. (As Lyndon Johnson would have put it, it was better to have Saddam "inside the tent pissing out than outside pissing in.")

Accordingly, Americans, and the rest of the world as well,

were treated to the spectacle of the now-infamous April Glaspie interview, in which the Iraqi dictator was assured by the U.S. ambassador that we were not about to take a position on intra-Arab disputes, such as Saddam's claims on Kuwait. That Ambassador Glaspie's message to Saddam—both the text and the subtext—was of a piece with views long prevalent in the State Department's Bureau of Near Eastern Affairs did not mitigate the damage done by the administration on this front. For it was within the administration's power, particularly as the Cold War was declining and the unipolar nature of power in the world was coming into clearer focus, to challenge the appeasement strategies that State had been urging, precisely in the name of creating conditions (psychological as well as political-military) more conducive to the pursuit of a genuine peace.

That the president and his men responded so forcefully to a crisis that they had, in part, helped bring about is to their credit. It is easy to imagine several of the Democratic candidates in 1988 adopting precisely the pre–August 1990 approach taken by the Bush administration, and then, after the invasion of Kuwait, waiting for sanctions to work. And waiting. And waiting. The Bush administration did, not just the expedient thing, but the right thing in mounting Desert Shield and Desert Storm. And the decision to eject Saddam from Kuwait by military means if necessary was couched in precisely the right terms: as a matter of obligation as well as of necessity.

But then, with Saddam hanging on to power by the thinnest of threads, Bush's policy lurched back to the orthodoxies of conventional realism. To be sure, there was a concern within senior administration circles that the relentless pursuit of the Iraqi army out of Basra would have led to a breach of the just-war principle of proportionality. But there were options between what amounted to a unilateral ceasefire and rolling the tanks up to Baghdad. Moreover, it seems ever more obvious that the endgame policy was being driven by other concerns: by, once again, concerns about stability.

The Saudis were reported to be nervous about the break-up of Iraq and the possible creation of a Shiite state (or autonomous region) in southern Iraq. So, it was said, were the Turks—with the Kurds as the potential problem child in the north of Iraq, along the Turkish border. The decision was, therefore, made to stop military action; to preserve the Iraq state and the Baathist regime in their present form; and to hope that, somehow, Saddam would be removed from power by the normal means for the transfer of power in the Middle East: assassination and/or coup.

But when that hope proved vain, the administration was even prepared to let Saddam and his Baathist thugs slaughter Shiites and Kurds by the tens of thousands in the name of preserving the stability that a unitary Iraq, under Baathist leadership, would putatively help create in the region. Charles Krauthammer put it sharply but accurately when he wrote in *Time* (October 14, 1991) that Bush's "first choice was Saddamism without Saddam. But his second choice was Saddamism with Saddam." The reason for that otherwise inexplicable choice was that it was demanded by the administration's version of conventional realism. (Irony of ironies, Saddam Hussein remained in power to celebrate publicly, November 4, 1992, the electoral defeat of his antagonist.)

Yugoslavia

If Yugoslavia—a nation-state in name only, a misbegotten child of the Versailles Peace Conference that came apart under the inexorable pressures generated by the Communist manipulation of ancient ethnic and religious feuds—graphically illustrated the enduring perils of Wilsonianism, Bush administration policy toward that unhappy land was a poignant reminder that the fundamental principle of sound diplomacy remains the same as the basic principle of sound medicine: first, do no harm.

That Yugoslavia was in dire straits, indeed on the verge of civil war, by the summer of 1991 ought to have been evident to any informed observer. Yet Secretary of State Baker went to Belgrade in June of that year and defined the United States' interest in Yugoslavia as the maintenance of stability and order. Not without reason, this was seen by the Serbian Communists then in control of the Yugoslav federal leadership and the federal army as a signal that the United States would not object to a little head-knocking, if that was what it would take to preserve the unitary Yugoslav state. Shortly after Baker's visit, Ljubljana became the first European city to be bombed since 1945. And the catastrophes visited on Dubrovnik and Sarajevo were not far behind, nor were the barbarities of "ethnic cleansing."

Could the United States have prevented a civil war in Yugoslavia? Perhaps not. But Baker's ill-advised emphasis on stability made civil war more, not less, likely. Worse yet, it strengthened the hand of the very man who had been the chief obstacle to a peaceful resolution of the Yugoslav dilemma, the Serbian Stalinist Slobodan Milosevic. Had Baker stressed that America's interest lay in a peaceful, democratic, nonviolent, and negotiated settlement of the crisis (even if that meant a radical restructuring of "Yugoslavia"), and had he challenged the Yugoslavs to emulate the success of their Slavic brethren in carrying out just such revolutions in Poland and Czechoslovakia, things just might have been different. Instead, two years after the Revolution of 1989, we gave effective support to one of the few remaining Communist leaders in Eastern Europe. The bloodletting followed in short order.

Gorbachev, Yeltsin, and the August Revolution

Stability, rather than democracy and nonviolent change, was, yet again, the watchword for the Bush administration's policy toward the Soviet Union during its death throes. That policy was also shaped in considerable part by Bush's evident fondness for Mikhail Gorbachev, and his advisers' nervousness about the less "clubbable" Boris Yeltsin. But the element of personality does not fully account for the way in which Bush came down strongly on the side of Gorbachev's centralist reform Communism in the paradigmatic formulation of the administration's pre–August 1991 Revolution perspective—his August 1 address to the Ukrainian parliament in Kiev, which William Safire of the *New York Times* acidly dubbed the "Chicken Kiev speech." That speech, with its dire warnings against the perils of "suicidal nationalism," may well appear, in time, to have been the most comprehensive statement of the conventional-realist position—and the most telling example of that position's failure to grasp the meaning and power of the ideas and passions that drove politics during the break-up of the external and internal Soviet empires.

The pattern established by the Chicken Kiev speech was maintained throughout the August 1991 Revolution. In the early going, the president was just right: calm, measured, quietly defiant. But in the wake of Yeltsin's victory in Moscow, Bush seemed as little able as Gorbachev to comprehend that a sea-change had taken place in the correlation of forces within what was rapidly becoming the former USSR. Once again, the rhetorical weight was on stability, with virtually no presidential acknowledgment that what was under way throughout the Soviet Union was a great triumph for Western political values. The president did celebrate the triumph of democracy when the coup imploded. But he immediately went on to suggest, against the evidence of Gorbachev's own astonishing press conference (in which he defended the Communist party he would abandon twenty-four hours later), that "democracy" and "Gorbachev" were somehow synonymous. Then there was the president's petulance about the demands for diplomatic recognition that came from the Baltic states, his deprecatory references to Ukrainian democrats, and his staffers' off-the-record trashing of Boris Yeltsin as a crude and unstable demagogue who gravely threatened, yes, the supreme value of stability.

In the weeks following the August Revolution, as in his phone-a-thon prior to the September 1991 announcement of nuclear-weapons cuts, the president moved toward a recognition of Yeltsin's position and stature as, minimally, co-leader with Gorbachev of whatever-it-was that the late Soviet Union had become. Then, in late November and early December, Gorbachev's inability to meet his payroll and the voters of Ukraine finally forced the administration's hand. But until then, it was the Chicken Kiev speech, with its stress on the importance of maintaining "the center" (at precisely the moment when the center was being revealed as a fiction), that was the intellectual template against which post-Soviet U.S. policy toward the collapsing superpower was measured and cut for far too long a time.

Some might argue that this cautious approach to the post-Soviet endgame—as well as to the events in Tiananmen Square, during the last phase of Desert Storm, and on the brink of the Yugoslav civil war—was but the application of that chief of political virtues, prudence, to policy-making in a volatile period in world affairs.

Yet what the Bush administration imagined to have been the prudent call in these four instances proved to be anything but: if by prudence we mean the skill of applying principle to practice in a way that allows for the maximum possible embodiment of that principle in the political order, given the limits imposed by circumstances. The People's Republic of China became a more repressive place, further removed from reform and just as troublesome in the world arms markets, in the wake of the administration's tepid response to the Tiananmen Square shootings. Saddam Hussein is still in power in Baghdad, and is still pursuing a nuclear-weapons capability: this is stability? Yugoslavia has been destroyed in civil war. And the United States seemed increasingly out of touch with events and personalities in the post–Soviet Union. In sum, given the revolutionary circumstances with which our policy had to come to grips, the stress the Bush administration put on stability was precisely the *imprudent* call.

The Defects of Conventional Realism

The Bush administration's imprudent pursuit of a "prudent" foreign policy illustrates the first of the three chief defects of conventional realism: its inability to deliver success, even (or especially) as measured by its own definition of success. Conventional realism rightly promises no rose gardens; but it does promise that diplomacy can produce stability and order, which is the best that can be hoped for in this kind of world. And yet, as the record of the Bush administration shows, it is precisely stability that conventional realism fails to produce. The root of that failure lies in conventional realism's blindness to the power of ideas—of ideology—in world politics, and the capacity of peoples motivated by ideas and moral passions to bend history to their wills. Thanks to this crippling myopia (which is rooted in the belief that the world of ideas is epiphenomenal to the "real world" of economics and military power), conventional realism missed the *sine qua non* of the Revolution of 1989 in Central and Eastern Europe and the August 1991 Revolution in the late Soviet Union: the revolution of the spirit, the revolution of conscience, that preceded and made possible the (largely nonviolent) over-throw of Communist power.

This grave weakness in the intellectual armamentarium of conventional realism should not surprise anyone familiar with the diplomatic history of the twentieth century. Conventional realists were, after all, in charge at 10 Downing Street and in the French Foreign Ministry when the most urgent questions of the day were: who is Hitler and what does he want? Conventional realism, incapable of grasping revolutionary ide-ologies and passions, fundamentally misconstrued Hitler, who, it was said, had legitimate, post-Versailles grievances that could be redressed by "appeasement" (a good word, then). The same incapacity to comprehend the revolutionary mind-set, this time in the case of Stalin, crippled Western strategy and diplomacy from the Teheran conference through Yalta.

The second failure of conventional realism is its misunder-standing of morality, and particularly of the moral reasoning appropriate to statecraft. Conventional realism, with its pre-tense of tough-mindedness, denies that the world of politics has a normative content: politics is, at best, amoral, and international politics is even more the arena of the amoral than domestic affairs. The only calculus that counts in foreign policy is a calculus of national interest, and those charged with the responsibility of securing that interest are somehow thought to have been absolved from grappling with the ques-tion, But what *ought* we to do? At its most perfervid, conven-tional realism even imputes a kind of stoic grandeur to the lonely amoralism of the statesman; as the eminent realist Hans Morgenthau once put it, "To know with despair that the political act is inevitably evil, and to act nevertheless, is moral courage."

In fact, however, this is not moral courage but rather a particularly offensive form of melodramatics. The philosopher

Charles Frankel took Morgenthau to task for his bloviated formulation at just the right level of analysis:

> Professor Morgenthau is pointing only to the fact that man cannot have or do everything he wants, that he must choose, and that he must do so though inadequately informed and equipped. To turn these not entirely recondite facts into evidence for the proposition that politics is no place for ethics is a resounding non sequitur. Human fallibility and choice are not evil. They are the conditions that make the moral life, and therefore both good and evil, possible.

Conventional realism is, then, defective as a moral theory. It considers the norms appropriate for decision-making in interpersonal relationships the sum total of the meaning of morality and then, finding these inapplicable in politics among nations, declares foreign policy to be the realm of the amoral calculation of interest. In this, conventional realism resembles (and in fact probably derives in no small part from) that form of American evangelical Protestant moralism that drove a wedge between morality and politics by insisting that the former was solely derivative from the norms of the Sermon on the Mount. But as the vigorous "just war" debate that preceded Desert Storm illustrated, there are other sources of moral understanding—preeminent among them the natural law—and these can provide far more supple instruments for serious moral analysis of the exigencies of statecraft.

Finally, on this point, the conventional realists' insistence that the national interest is the sole concern of the statesman tends to ignore the fact that the calculation of what constitutes the national interest is itself an exercise in moral judgment, not an exercise in algebra. It inevitably involves choices among desiderata, choices that are inescapably involved with issues of "ought." Once again, it was Charles Frankel who got this exactly right:

The heart of the decision-making process . . . is not the finding of the best means to serve a national interest already perfectly known and understood. It is the determining of that interest itself: the reassessment of the nation's resources, needs, commitments, traditions, and political and cultural horizons—in short, its calendar of values.

Conventional realism of the European/*realpolitik* sort is thus not an escape from morality; it is a defective and deficient form of morality. Nor is the alternative to conventional realism utopianism or idealism run amok. The alternative is better moral reasoning. It is an approach to the construction of foreign policy that grasps ideas and values as motivators of men and nations; that takes seriously the distinctive nature of social ethics, and particularly its necessary concern for consequences; and that does not throw up its hands in despair over the inevitable fact that there is going to be a gap between our ideals and their implementation in the doing of our business with the world.

The third disability of conventional realism is its incapacity to engage the imagination and commitment of the American people. Conventional realism does not suit the political temper of a people whose constituting experience as a political community involved the assertion of universal moral norms. A nation founded on ideas and values cannot but make those ideas and values a formative part of its encounter with the world.

Margaret Thatcher used to distinguish between "conviction politicians" and "consensus politicians." The United States, for good and for ill and usually for both, is a conviction nation. Our convictions cannot determine policy in all particulars. There are limits to our capabilities, and there are limits posed by the intractabilities of situations, cultures, and personalities in the world. On occasion, for example, we may have to enter (or even lead) coalitions with partners whose polities we find odious.

But the real danger is not that we will somehow lose our innocence in such ventures. Americans are not so naive as that. Moreover, the arguments of the democratic internationalists, given added weight by the empirical evidence of democracy's power as an energizing principle in politics within and among nations, and sharpened by the cautions of the more developed realist thinkers like Kristol, Harries, Kissinger, and Kirkpatrick, will continue to offer a potent analytic framework for conceiving ways to bridge the inevitable gaps between what our convictions would lead us to want to do, and what the circumstances of a given situation require of us.

Contrary to much assumed wisdom (of the kind that thinks of itself as tough-minded and pragmatic, rather than idealistic and ideological), the fact of those gaps is no reason to fall back into the false intellectual and political safety net of conventional realism. Indeed, the real danger in the early 1990s was that the Bush administration's experiments and principle-free *realpolitik* would so estrange our foreign policy from the deepest convictions of the American people that they would decide to retreat in disgust (or, at the very least, confusion) into the kind of hemispheric bunker designed by Buchanan and his tribe. The great irony, of course, is that the conventional realism of an administration that prided itself on its expertise in dealing with the world could have become a new road—the upmarket road—to the very isolationism it sought to avoid. That has not happened: yet. But the dangers of it were still alive in 1993 when the Clinton administration took office, in a world where the problems of violent conflict continued to demand serious attention and imaginative statecraft.

Response

Luis E. Lugo

The sharp wit, engaging style, penetrating analysis, and high moral purpose that characterize George Weigel's writings contribute significantly to the level of political discourse in this country. My favorable estimation of Weigel's work, of course, also has something to do with what I believe to be the basic soundness of his political approach. His critique of the conventional-realist position is a good case in point. The proposition that morality could somehow be divorced from international affairs should strike any right-thinking person as deeply suspect. No political decision, whether in domestic or foreign policy, can be made independently of certain moral judgments. Thus Weigel reasons correctly that conventional realism, far from representing a complete repudiation of the normative element in world politics, is itself but a defective moral theory.

I admit, however, that I am somewhat more sympathetic than Weigel to realist concerns. Realists reacted to a conventional idealism that, with easy optimism, failed to recognize the abiding relevance of power considerations in the pursuit of moral ends in international politics. Moreover, realists rightly rejected the idealist tendency to divorce international morality from the very practical and legitimate interests of the

---

Luis E. Lugo teaches in the political science department at Calvin College in Michigan.

United States. Wilson's contention that we fought World War I "for the universal dominion of right," quite apart from any concrete American interests, overlooks the obvious fact that protecting legitimate national interests carries a certain moral dignity. To approach international conflicts in "a purely ethical light," as C. S. Lewis reminded us, "is a step down, not up" in moral reasoning. A concomitant of Wilson's insufferable self-righteousness, this kind of idealism tended to impart a false transcendence to "things that are very much part of this world." This is a mindset that is always in danger of losing the crucial distinction between just wars and holy wars.[1]

But such qualifications do not alter the basic fact that I fundamentally agree with Weigel and consider him an ally in this country's emerging foreign-policy battles. Weigel rightly observes that the end of the Cold War has opened a debate that goes to the very heart of the question of what ought to be the proper role of the United States in the world. And he correctly senses that the greatest challenge in this back-to-first-principles debate comes from a reinvigorated isolationist camp. Alan Tonelson, whose utter pragmatism prevents him from viewing even the policy of nonintervention as a binding moral principle, has stated the argument for that side most pointedly—and perhaps also most crudely. Under his brand of isolationism, Tonelson informs us, policy-makers "would be free to use whatever approach or combination of approaches seemed likeliest to achieve the best ends for the United States in a given situation. Its only rule of thumb would be 'whatever works' to preserve or enhance America's security and prosperity."[2] Doug Bandow's call for a policy of "benign detachment," though more moderate in tone and more principled in character, rests on fairly similar assumptions.[3]

Given the end of the Soviet threat and our deep-seated domestic problems, it is only prudent, of course, that we rethink U.S. foreign policy. Many specific policy proposals of the isolationist camp do, in fact, make very good sense. The new isolationism, however, calls into question the essential solidarity (used here in the Catholic rather than the Marxist sense) of the human community by making national boundaries the absolute outer limits of moral obligations. A fellow Spaniard, Francisco Suarez, provided a cogent response to that idea: "No matter how a sovereign state, commonwealth or kingdom may be in itself a perfect society with its own members, each one is also, in a sense, as seen from the point of view of the human race, a member of the universal human community."[4] There are, indeed, political duties beyond national borders. On this, Weigel and I are quite agreed.

On a more practical policy level, I join Weigel in his praise of some aspects of the Bush administration's foreign policy, as well as in his criticism of some others. Not the least of Weigel's criticisms is his contention that the Bush administration was not only skeptical of great principles in the conduct of foreign policy but lacked an adequate appreciation of the role of ideas in world affairs. Bush's New World Order was, alas, a largely vacuous notion. But Weigel should remember that Bush was, after all, the president of a country whose major contribution to the history of Western philosophy is the philosophy of pragmatism.

Unfortunately, as Weigel suggests, the discipline of international politics has not provided the much-needed corrective to this American aversion to the world of ideas. American political science seems only to reinforce the inherent tendencies in American foreign policy. Its uncritical attempt to emulate natural-science methodologies has served to undermine the discipline's classical concern with the truly important moral/philosophical questions of statecraft. There may be grounds for optimism, however. At a recent meeting of the American Political Science Association, a panel composed of some leading lights from places like Stanford, Harvard, and Cornell announced, with nary a hint of embarrassment, that they had now discovered that such ideas as sovereignty and human rights do indeed have practical consequences.

Understanding Pragmatism

But the contention that the pragmatism of the Bush administration marked a clear departure from the foreign policy of the previous administration needs to be examined more closely. The Reagan Doctrine, in my view, did not represent a simple, straightforward commitment to the promotion of democracy throughout the world. Looking at it in more traditional geopolitical terms, one can easily discern a reworked version of the failed rollback doctrine of the 1950s, now applied, with more success, to the periphery of the Soviet empire. Though I supported the Nicaraguan resistance and the UNITA rebels, it never occurred to me that Enrique Bermudez or Jonas Savimbi—nevermind the Afghan guerrilla leaders—should be held up as model democratic statesmen. One could go further and suggest that the Reagan Doctrine was no less morally ambiguous than the previous Kirkpatrick Doctrine.[5] Charles Krauthammer was right when he argued in defense of the Reagan Doctrine that "there are no moral foxholes," that sometimes our choice is between the lesser of two evils. This is certainly true, but it is also an acknowledgement that support for democracy was not the primary focus of the policy.[6]

Be that as it may, Weigel does point to a very real danger: concern for order and stability can easily lead to an overly cautious foreign policy that fails to promote important moral objectives and that can, paradoxically, end up undermining itself. Those who must be cautious should at least avoid being too cynical, a maxim that we clearly violated in our response to the events surrounding Tiananmen Square. But the Bush administration deserves a word or two of defense on this question of caution.

First, it is inherent in the world of politics that those who shoulder the burden of public office will be more hesitant to depart from established policy than those of us on the outside. Even when they, like us, sense new possibilities, prudent concerns about potential risks invariably serve to strengthen the hand of advisers who counsel a more moderate course. Interestingly, Weigel's criticism here is reminiscent of that directed at the Pentagon by the American Left during the turbulent 1980s. The argument then was that the Reagan administration was not sufficiently aggressive in pursuing new possibilities in U.S.-Soviet relations—achieving more extensive arms-control agreements, for example. While one is always able to imagine better futures, one should also keep in mind, as policy-makers generally do, that worse futures are also possible.

Second, Weigel too easily dismisses the notion that the search for stability in an anarchic system of world politics carries a certain moral weight. A minimum of order is, after all, the precondition for the attainment of higher moral ends. And the history of modern international politics should teach us not to underestimate the difficulty of achieving even this minimum degree of order. The abiding challenge to good statesmanship, of course, is to go beyond this minimal level of coexistence and achieve something that can more properly be called a just order. In doing so, however, we should keep in mind Hedley Bull's wise counsel that "it is better to begin with the elements of world order that actually exist, and consider how they might be cultivated."[7]

Weigel is well aware that the last few years have witnessed some rather remarkable transformations in world affairs. The end of the bipolarity that characterized the Cold War period is only the most obvious. The increasing attraction of democratic capitalism throughout the world, including my native Latin America, is another important change. Both these changes might suggest that the next stage in the natural development of the global system will be a new era of unipolarity, of a pax Americana. But the careful observer will also be impressed by the increasing multipolarity in world affairs, most prominently in global economic affairs.

The Gulf War highlighted both tendencies in a most poignant fashion. Here was an overwhelmingly successful exercise of U.S. military might—financed entirely by foreign capital! There is simply no escaping the hard fact that our economic standing relative to the other major players on the world stage has weakened considerably in recent years. As a result, the United States may be less prepared to manage the coming geoeconomic challenges of our erstwhile allies than we were to confront the geopolitical challenges of our erstwhile enemies. The Bush administration has faced—and the Clinton administration will likewise face—the difficult task of learning to live in a very different world. Erring on the side of caution in this turbulent environment seems to me quite understandable, even if not completely satisfactory.

Weigel's impatience with the Bush administration record, however, seems to go much deeper than particular disagreements over specific policies. His critique is rooted ultimately in a certain view of the democratic project, which he takes to be both inevitable and sufficient to define the direction of U.S. foreign policy. I should like to raise some questions concerning both of these assumptions.

Is Democracy Enough?

When Weigel takes the measure of the present global situation, he discovers that a democratic revolution of major proportions is taking place all around us. By focusing too closely on military and economic power, he argues, the Bush administration did a grave injustice to the contemporary democratic zeitgeist. For Weigel the policy choice appears to boil down to this: either pursue stability and order or promote democracy and nonviolent change. He seems to assume that nonviolent democratic revolutions will almost inevitably follow in the wake of change.

But how can Weigel be so sure that democratic forces rather than other less attractive alternatives, such as neofascism or ultranationalism, will emerge victorious? We all hope, of course, that his assumption is correct, but the present reality should give us pause. Weigel's very optimistic, almost triumphalist, reading of the current world situation must be influenced by progressivist assumptions that he never makes explicit. His reading of the signs of the times seems to be under the spell of Hegel's ghost, at least as mediated through Francis Fukuyama. I am reminded here of the liberation theologians of Latin America, who, during those repressive years of military-authoritarian rule, read the signs of the times to require of God's people support for the Marxist-inspired guerrilla insurgencies that then seemed on the march throughout the continent. As we all know, history was more difficult to exegete than those theologians ever imagined.

Perhaps Lord Acton is a more reliable guide in this connection. That great nineteenth-century Catholic historian saw that "the achievement of liberty was the thread of progress to be discerned in human history." But that same human history, he warned, "was also a solid rebuke to sanguine presumptions about the nature and the future of man."[8]

Even if one were to concede that the democratic revolution is both universal and irreversible, one must still ask whether the promotion of democracy is a sufficient basis for U.S. policy. To argue that it is raises some rather curious questions. If the promotion of democracy is the central norm of foreign policy, for example, are we to believe that foreign policy was essentially normless prior to the age when democracy became a global historical option? Moreover, what shall serve as our guide in the conduct of foreign relations once democracy has been established on a global basis? Or are we to assume that a world of democratic nations will finally escape all the problems that have bedeviled countries in the past? If there are no norms more central to interstate relations than the promotion of democracy, then the triumph of democracy will surely mark the end of history, at least of international history as we have known it. But if, indeed, there are norms for U.S. foreign policy more central than playing the role of midwife in this worldwide process of democratization, Weigel has not told us.

I suspect that he must have something in mind, for if the history of even this greatest of democracies is at all instructive, we must surely conclude that democracy is no ultimate guarantee of justice. Under this democracy, for instance, slavery was legal for nearly a century, and under this democracy millions of the most helpless members of the human community are to this very day denied their God-given right to life. Moreover, the spread of democracy can also be quite compatible with an attack on basic human freedoms. Already in the early nineteenth century, Tocqueville warned us of a "democratic despotism" that combines popular sovereignty with the increasing power of the administrative state.[9]

And what holds for domestic policy also holds for foreign policy. Though no great critic of U.S.–Latin American policy, I can certainly point to more than one instance of U.S. military intervention in the region that one would be hard-pressed to justify on classical just-war grounds. Even a world of democratic countries, then, cannot guarantee that either domestic or foreign affairs will be ordered in a just manner. Thus, I contend that we still need to clarify the basic norms of international life. Only then will we be able to hold (even) democratic countries to a higher standard. Weigel calls for a social ethics that is morally more compelling than the defective morality of *realpolitik*. While I should very much like to join him in this quest, I wonder if he and the democratic internationalists have offered us a genuine alternative. Is democracy enough?

PART II

The Prudence Tradition

1

From Aristotle,
Nichomachean Ethics

*The following excerpt is taken from Book VI, 1139b–1145a,
translated by W. D. Ross.*

Let it be assumed that the states by virtue of which the soul
possesses truth by way of affirmation or denial are five in
number, i.e. art, scientific knowledge, practical wisdom [or
prudence*], philosophic wisdom, intuitive reason; we do not
include judgment and opinion because in these we may be
mistaken. . . .

Regarding *practical wisdom* we shall get at the truth by
considering who are the persons we credit with it. Now it is
thought to be the mark of a man of practical wisdom to be
able to deliberate well about what is good and expedient for
himself, not in some particular respect, e.g. about what sorts
of thing conduce to health or to strength, but about what
sorts of thing conduce to the good life in general. This is
shown by the fact that we credit men with practical wisdom
in some particular respect when they have calculated well with
a view to some good end which is one of those that are not

---

*In many translations, "practical wisdom" and "prudence" are used
interchangeably for the Greek term *phronesis*.

99

the object of any art. It follows that in the general sense also the man who is capable of deliberating has practical wisdom. Now no one deliberates about things that are invariable, nor about things that it is impossible for him to do. Therefore, since scientific knowledge involves demonstration, but there is no demonstration of things whose first principles are variable (for all such things might actually be otherwise), and since it is impossible to deliberate about things that are of necessity, practical wisdom cannot be scientific knowledge nor art; not science because that which can be done is capable of being otherwise, not art because action and making are different kinds of thing. The remaining alternative, then, is that it is a true and reasoned state of capacity to act with regard to the things that are good or bad for man. For while making has an end other than itself, action cannot; for good action itself is its end.

It is for this reason that we think Pericles and men like him have practical wisdom, viz. because they can see what is good for themselves and what is good for men in general; we consider that those can do this who are good at managing households or states. (This is why we call temperance, *sophrosyne*, by this name; we imply that it preserves one's practical wisdom, *sodsousa ten phronesin*. Now what it preserves is a judgment of the kind we have described. For it is not any and every judgment that pleasant and painful objects destroy and pervert, e.g. the judgment that the triangle has or has not its angles equal to two right angles, but only judgments about what is to be done. For the originating causes of the things that are done consist in the end at which they are aimed; but the man who has been ruined by pleasure or pain forthwith fails to see any such originating cause—to see that for the sake of this or because of this he ought to choose and do whatever he chooses and does; for vice is destructive of the originating cause of action.)

Practical wisdom, then, must be a reasoned and true state of capacity to act with regard to human goods. But further, while there is such a thing as excellence in art, there is no such thing as excellence in practical wisdom; and in art he who errs willingly is preferable, but in practical wisdom, as in the virtues, he is the reverse. Plainly, then, practical wisdom is a virtue and not an art. There being two parts of the soul that can follow a course of reasoning, it must be the virtue of one of the two, i.e. of that part which forms opinions; for opinion is about the variable and so is practical wisdom. But yet it is not only a reasoned state; this is shown by the fact that a state of that sort may be forgotten but practical wisdom cannot.

Scientific knowledge is judgment about things that are universal and necessary, and the conclusions of demonstration, and all scientific knowledge, follow from first principles (for scientific knowledge involves apprehension of a rational ground). This being so, the first principle from which what is scientifically known follows cannot be an object of scientific knowledge, of art, or of practical wisdom; for that which can be scientifically known can be demonstrated, and art and practical wisdom deal with things that are variable. Nor are these first principles of objects of philosophic wisdom, for it is a mark of the philosopher to have *demonstration* about some things. If, then, the states of mind by which we have truth and are never deceived about things invariable or even variable are scientific knowledge, practical wisdom, philosophic wisdom, and intuitive reason, and it cannot be any of the three (i.e. practical wisdom, scientific knowledge, or philosophic wisdom), the remaining alternative is that it is *intuitive reason* that grasps the first principles.

Wisdom (1) in the arts we ascribe to their most finished exponents, e.g. to Phidias as a sculptor and to Polyclitus as a maker of portrait-statues, and here we mean nothing by wisdom except excellence in art; but (2) we think that some people are wise in general, not in some particular field or in any other limited respect, as Homer says in the *Margites*,

> Him did the gods make neither a digger not yet a
> ploughman
> Nor wise in anything else.

Therefore wisdom must plainly be the most finished of the forms of knowledge. It follows that the wise man must not only know what follows from the first principles, but must also possess truth about the first principles. Therefore wisdom must be intuitive reason combined with scientific knowledge—scientific knowledge of the highest objects which has received as it were its proper completion.

Of the highest objects, we say; for it would be strange to think that the art of politics, or practical wisdom, is the best knowledge, since man is not the best thing in the world. Now if what is healthy or good is different for men and for fishes, but what is white or straight is always the same, any one would say that what is wise is the same but what is practically wise is different; for it is to that which observes well the various matters concerning itself that one ascribes practical wisdom, and it is to this that one will entrust such matters. This is why we say that some even of the lower animals have practical wisdom, viz. those which are found to have a power of foresight with regard to their own life. It is evident also that philosophic wisdom and the art of politics cannot be the same; for if the state of mind concerned with a man's own interests is to be called philosophic wisdom, there will be many philosophic wisdoms; there will not be one concerned with the good of all animals (any more than there is one art of medicine for all existing things), but a different philosophic wisdom about the good of each species.

But if the argument be that man is the best of the animals, this makes no difference; for there are other things much more divine in their nature even than man, e.g., most conspicuously, the bodies of which the heavens are framed. From what has been said it is plain, then, that philosophic wisdom is scientific knowledge, combined with intuitive reason, of the things that are highest by nature. This is why we say Anaxagoras, Thales, and men like them have philosophic but not practical wisdom, when we see them ignorant of what is to their own advantage, and why we say that they know things that are remarkable, admirable, difficult, and divine, but useless; viz. because it is not human goods that they seek.

Practical wisdom on the other hand is concerned with things human and things about which it is possible to deliberate; for we say this is above all the work of the man of practical wisdom, to deliberate well, but no one deliberates about things invariable, nor about things which have not an end, and that a good that can be brought about by action. The man who is without qualification good at deliberating is the man who is capable of aiming in accordance with calculation at the best for man of things attainable by action. Nor is practical wisdom concerned with universals only—it must also recognize the particulars; for it is practical, and practice is concerned with particulars. This is why some who do not know, and especially those who have experience, are more practical than others who know; for if a man knew that light meats are digestible and wholesome, but did not know which sorts of meat are light, he would not produce health, but the man who knows that chicken is wholesome is more likely to produce health.

Now practical wisdom is concerned with action; therefore one should have both forms of it, or the latter in preference to the former. But of practical as of philosophic wisdom there must be a controlling kind.

Political wisdom and practical wisdom are the same state of mind, but their essence is not the same. Of the wisdom concerned with the city, the practical wisdom which plays a controlling part is legislative wisdom, while that which is related to this as particulars to their universal is known by the general name "political wisdom"; this has to do with action and deliberation, for a decree is a thing to be carried out in the form of an individual act. This is why the exponents of this art are alone said to "take part in politics"; for these alone "do things" as manual laborers "do things".

Practical wisdom also is identified especially with that form of it which is concerned with a man himself—with the individual; and this is known by the general name "practical wisdom"; of the other kinds one is called household management, another legislation, the third politics, and of the latter one part is called deliberative and the other judicial. Now knowing what is good for oneself will be one kind of knowledge, but it is very different from the other kinds; and the man who knows and concerns himself with his own interests is thought to have practical wisdom, while politicians are thought to be busybodies; hence the words of Euripides,

> But how could I be wise, who might at ease,
> Numbered among the army's multitude,
> Have had an equal share? . . .
> For those who aim too high and do too much. . . .

Those who think thus seek their own good, and consider that one ought to do so. From this opinion, then, has come the view that such men have practical wisdom; yet perhaps one's own good cannot exist without household management, nor without a form of government. Further, how one should order one's own affairs is not clear and needs inquiry.

What has been said is confirmed by the fact that while young men become geometricians and mathematicians and wise in matters like these, it is thought that a young man of practical wisdom cannot be found. The cause is that such wisdom is concerned not only with universals but with particulars, which become familiar from experience, but a young man has no experience, for it is length of time that gives experience; indeed one might ask this question too, why a boy may become a mathematician, but not a philosopher or a physicist. Is it because the objects of mathematics exist by abstraction, while the first principles of these other subjects come from experience, and because young men have no conviction about the latter but merely use the proper language, while the essence of mathematical objects is plain enough to them?

Further, error in deliberation may be either about the universal or about the particular; we may fail to know either that all water that weighs heavy is bad, or that this particular water weighs heavy.

That practical wisdom is not scientific knowledge is evident; for it is, as has been said, concerned with the ultimate particular fact, since the thing to be done is of this nature. It is opposed, then, to intuitive reason; for intuitive reason is of the limiting premises, for which no reason can be given, while practical wisdom is concerned with the ultimate particular, which is the object not of scientific knowledge but of perception—not the perception of qualities peculiar to one sense but a perception akin to that by which we perceive that the particular figure before us is a triangle; for in that direction as well as in that of the major premise there will be a limit. But this is rather perception than practical wisdom, though it is another kind of perception than that of the qualities peculiar to each sense.

There is a difference between inquiry and deliberation; for deliberation is inquiry into a particular kind of thing. We must grasp the nature of excellence in deliberation as well—whether it is a form of scientific knowledge, or opinion, or skill in conjecture, or some other kind of thing. *Scientific knowledge* it is not; for men do not inquire about the things they know about, but good deliberation is a kind of deliberation, and he who deliberates inquires and calculates. Nor is it *skill in conjecture*; for this both involves no reasoning and is something that is quick in its operation, while men deliberate a long time, and they say that one should carry out quickly the conclusions of one's deliberation, but should deliberate slowly. Again, *readiness of mind* is different from excellence in deliberation; it is a sort of skill in conjecture. Nor again is excellence in deliberation *opinion* of any sort. But since the man who deliberates badly makes a mistake, while he who deliberates well does so correctly, excellence in deliberation is clearly a kind of correctness, but neither of knowledge nor of opinion; for there is no such thing as correctness of knowledge (since there is no such thing as error of knowledge), and correctness of opinion is truth; and at the same time everything that is an object of opinion is already determined. But again excellence in deliberation involves reasoning. The remaining alternative, then, is that it is *correctness of thinking*; for this is not yet assertion, since, while even opinion is not inquiry but has reached the stage of assertion, the man who is deliberating, whether he does so well or ill, is searching for something and calculating.

But excellence in deliberation is a certain correctness of deliberation; hence we must first inquire what deliberation is and what it is about. And, there being more than one kind of correctness, plainly excellence in deliberation is not any and every kind; for (1) the incontinent man and the bad man, if he is clever, will reach as a result of his calculation what he sets before himself, so that he will have deliberated correctly, but he will have got for himself a great evil. Now to have deliberated well is thought to be a good thing; for it is this kind of correctness of deliberation that is excellence in deliberation, viz. that which tends to attain what is good. But (2) it is possible to attain even good by a false syllogism, and to attain what one ought to do but not by the right means, the middle term being false; so that this too is not yet excellence in deliberation—this state in virtue of which one attains what one ought but not by the right means. Again (3) it is possible to attain it by long deliberation while another man attains it quickly. Therefore in the former case we have not yet got excellence in deliberation, which is rightness with regard to the expedient—rightness in respect both of the end, the manner, and the time (4). Further it is possible to have deliberated well either in the unqualified sense or with reference to a particular end. Excellence in deliberation in the unqualified sense, then, is that which succeeds with reference to what is the end in the unqualified sense, and excellence in deliberation in a particular sense is that which succeeds relatively to a particular end. If, then, it is characteristic of men of practical wisdom to have deliberated well, excellence in deliberation will be correctness with regard to what conduces to the end of which practical wisdom is the true apprehension.

Understanding, also, and goodness of understanding, in virtue of which men are said to be men of understanding or of good understanding, are neither entirely the same as opinion or scientific knowledge (for at that rate all men would have been men of understanding), nor are they one of the particular sciences, such as medicine, the science of things connected with health, or geometry, the science of spatial magnitudes. For understanding is neither about things that are always and are unchangeable, nor about any and every one of the things that come into being, but about things which may become subjects of questioning and deliberation. Hence it is about the same objects as practical wisdom; but understanding and practical wisdom are not the same. For practical wisdom issues commands, since its end is what ought to be done or not to be done; but understanding only judges. (Understanding is identical with goodness of understanding, men of understanding with men of good understanding.) Now understanding is neither the having nor the acquiring of practical wisdom; but as learning is called understanding when it means the exercise of the faculty of knowledge, so "understanding" is applicable to the exercise of the faculty of opinion for the purpose of judging of what someone else says about matters with which practical wisdom is concerned—and of judging soundly; for "well" and "soundly" are the same thing. And from this has come the use of name "understanding" in virtue of which men are said to be "of good understanding," viz. from the application of the word to the grasping of scientific truth; for we often call such grasping understanding.

What is called judgment, in virtue of which men are said to "be sympathetic judges" and to "have judgment," is the right discrimination of the equitable. This is shown by the fact that we say the equitable man is above all others a man of sympathetic judgment, and identify equity with sympathetic judgment about certain facts. And sympathetic judgment is judgment which discriminates what is equitable and does so correctly; and correct judgment is that which judges what is true.

Now all the states we have considered converge, as might be expected, to the same point; for when we speak of judgment and understanding and practical wisdom and intuitive reason we credit the same people with possessing judgment and having reached years of reason and with having practical wisdom and understanding. For all these faculties deal with ultimates, i.e. with particulars; and being a man of understanding and of good or sympathetic judgment consists in being able to judge about the things with which practical wisdom is concerned; for the equities are common to all good men in relation to other men. Now all things which have to be done are included among particulars or ultimates; for not only must the man of practical wisdom know particular facts, but understanding and judgment are also concerned with things to be done, and these are ultimates. And intuitive reason is concerned with the ultimates in both directions; for both the first terms and the last are objects of intuitive reason and not of argument, and the intuitive reason which is presupposed by demonstrations grasps the unchangeable and first terms, while the intuitive reason involved in practical reasonings grasps the last and variable fact, i.e. the minor premise. For these variable facts are the starting points for the apprehension of the end, since the universals are reached from the particulars; of these therefore we must have perception, and this perception is intuitive reason.

This is why these states are thought to be natural endowments—why, while no one is thought to be a philosopher by nature, people are thought to have by nature judgment, understanding, and intuitive reason. This is shown by the fact that we think our powers correspond to our time of life, and that a particular age brings with it intuitive reason and judgment; this implies that nature is the cause. [Hence intuitive reason is both beginning and end; for demonstrations are from these and about these.] Therefore we ought to attend to the undemonstrated sayings and opinions of experienced and older people or of people of practical wisdom not less than to demonstrations; for because experience has given them an eye they see aright.

We have stated, then, what practical and philosophic wisdom are, and with what each of them is concerned, and we have said that each is the virtue of a different part of the soul.

Difficulties might be raised as to the utility of these qualities of mind. For (1) philosophic wisdom will contemplate none of the things that will make a man happy (for it is not concerned with any coming into being), and though practical wisdom has *this* merit, for what purpose do we need it? Practical wisdom is the quality of mind concerned with things just and noble and good for man, but these are the things which it is the mark of a *good* man to do, and we are none the more able to act for *knowing* them if the virtues are states of *character*, just as we are none the better able to act for knowing the things that are healthy and sound, in the sense not of producing but of issuing from the state of health; for we are none the more able to act for having the art of medicine or of gymnastics. But (2) if we are to say that a man should have practical wisdom not for the sake of knowing moral truths but for the sake of becoming good, practical wisdom will be of no use to those who *are* good; but again it is of no use to those who have *not* virtue; for it will make no difference whether they have practical wisdom themselves or obey others who have it, and it would be enough for us to do what we do in the case of health; though to wish to become healthy, yet we do not learn the art of medicine. (3) Besides this, it would be thought strange if practical wisdom, being inferior to philosophic wisdom, is to be put in authority over it, as seems to be implied by the fact that the art which produces anything rules and issues commands about that thing.

These, then, are the questions we must discuss; so far we have only stated the difficulties.

(1) Now first let us say that in themselves these states must be worthy of choice because they are the virtues of the two parts of the soul respectively, even if neither of them produces anything.

(2) Secondly, they do produce something, not as the art of

medicine produces health, however, but as health produces
health [i.e. as health, as an inner state, produces the activities
which we know as constituting health]; so does philosophic
wisdom produce happiness; for, being a part of virtue entire,
by being possessed and by actualizing itself it makes a man
happy.

(3) Again, the work of man is achieved only in accordance
with practical wisdom as well as with moral virtue; for virtue
makes us aim at the right mark, and practical wisdom makes
us take the right means. (Of the fourth part of the soul—the
nutritive [the other three being the scientific, the calculative,
and the desiderative]—there is no such virtue; for there is
nothing which it is in its power to do or not to do.)

(4) With regard to our being none the more able to do
because of our practical wisdom what is noble and just, let us
begin a little further back, starting with the following principle. As we say that some people who do just acts are not
necessarily just, i.e. those who do the acts ordained by the
laws either unwillingly or owing to ignorance or for some
other reason and not for the sake of the acts themselves
(though, to be sure, they do what they should and all the
things that the good man ought), so is it, it seems, that in
order to be good one must be in a certain state when one does
the several acts, i.e. one must do them as a result of choice and
for the sake of the acts themselves. Now virtue makes the
choice right, but the question of the things which should
naturally be done to carry out our choice belongs not to virtue
but to another faculty. We must devote our attention to these
matters and give a clearer statement about them. There is a
faculty which is called cleverness; and this is such as to be able
to do the things that tend toward the mark we have set before
ourselves, and to hit it. Now if the mark be noble, the
cleverness is laudable, but if the mark be bad, the cleverness is

mere smartness; hence we call even men of practical wisdom clever or smart. Practical wisdom is not the faculty, but it does not exist without this faculty. And this eye of the soul acquires its formed state not without the aid of virtue, as has been said and is plain; for the syllogisms which deal with acts to be done are things which involve a starting point, viz. "since the end, i.e. what is best, is of such and such a nature," whatever it may be (let it for the sake of argument be what we please); and this is not evident except to the good man; for wickedness perverts us and causes us to be deceived about the starting points of action. Therefore it it evident that it is impossible to be practically wise without being good.

We must therefore consider virtue also once more; for virtue too is similarly related; as practical wisdom is to cleverness— not the same, but like it—so is natural virtue to virtue in the strict sense. For all men think that each type of character belongs to its possessors in some sense by nature; for from the very moment of birth we are just or fitted for self-control or brave or have the other moral qualities; but yet we seek something else as that which is good in the strict sense—we seek for the presence of such qualities in another way. For both children and brutes have the natural dispositions to these qualities, but without reason these are evidently hurtful. Only we seem to see this much, that, while one may be led astray by them, as a strong body which moves without sight may stumble badly because of its lack of sight, still, if a man once acquires reason, that makes a difference in action; and his state, while still like what it was, will then be virtue in the strict sense. Therefore, as in the part of us which forms opinions there are two types, cleverness and practical wisdom, so too in the moral part there are two types, natural virtue and virtue in the strict sense, and of these the latter involves practical wisdom. This is why some say that all the virtues are forms of practical wisdom, and why Socrates in one respect was on the right track while in another he went astray; in thinking that all the virtues were forms of practical wisdom he was wrong, but in saying they implied practical wisdom he was right. This is confirmed by the fact that even now all men, when they define virtue, after naming the state of character and its objects add "that (state) which is in accordance with the right rule"; now the right rule is that which is in accordance with practical wisdom. All men, then, seem somehow to divine that this kind of state is virtue, viz. that which is in accordance with practical wisdom. But we must go a little further. For it is not merely the state in accordance with the right rule, but the state that implies the *presence* of the right rule, that is virtue; and practical wisdom is a right rule about such matters. Socrates, then, thought the virtues were rules or rational principles (for he thought they were, all of them, forms of scientific knowledge), while we think they *involve* a rational principle.

It is clear, then, from what has been said, that it is not possible to be good in the strict sense without practical wisdom, nor practically wise without moral virtue. But in this way we may also refute the dialectical argument whereby it might be contended that the virtues exist in separation from each other; the same man, it might be said, is not best equipped by nature for all the virtues, so that he will have already acquired one when he has not yet acquired another. This is possible in respect of the natural virtues, but not in respect of those in respect of which a man is called without qualification good; for with the presence of the one quality, practical wisdom, will be given all the virtues. And it is plain that, even if it were of no practical value, we should have needed it because it is the virtue of the part of us in question; plain too that the choice will not be right without practical wisdom any more than without virtue; for the one determines the end and the other makes us do the things that lead to the end.

But again it is not *supreme* over philosophic wisdom, i.e. over the superior part of us, any more than the art of medicine is over health; for it does not use it but provides for its coming into being; it issues orders, then, for its sake, but not to it. Further, to maintain its supremacy would be like saying that the art of politics rules the gods because it issues orders about all the affairs of the state.

2

From Thomas Aquinas, Summa Theologiae

The following excerpt is taken from the first English Dominican translation of the Second Part of the Second Part (II–II).

FROM QUESTION 47, ARTICLES 13 AND 14

Prudence is threefold. There is a false prudence, which takes its name from its likeness to true prudence. For since a prudent man is one who disposes well of the things that have to be done for a good end, whoever disposes well of such things as are fitting for an evil end, has false prudence, insofar as that which he takes for an end is good, not in truth but in appearance. Thus a man is called *a good robber,* and in this way we may speak of *a prudent robber,* by way of similarity, because he devises fitting ways of committing robbery. This is the prudence of which the Apostle [Paul] says (Rom. viii. 6): *The prudence* (Douay, *wisdom*) *of the flesh is death,* because, to wit, it places its ultimate end in the pleasures of the flesh.

The second prudence is indeed true prudence, because it devises fitting ways of obtaining a good end; and yet it is imperfect, from a twofold source. First, because the good which it takes for an end is not the common end of all human life, but of some particular affair; thus when a man devises

115

fitting ways of conducting business or of sailing a ship, he is called a prudent businessman, or a prudent sailor:—secondly, because he fails in the chief act of prudence, as when a man takes counsel aright, and forms a good judgment, even about things concerning life as a whole, but fails to make an effective command.

The third prudence is both true and perfect, for it takes counsel, judges and commands aright in respect of the good end of man's whole life: and this alone is prudence simply so-called, and cannot be in sinners, whereas the first prudence is in sinners alone, while imperfect prudence is common to good and wicked men, especially that which is imperfect through being directed to a particular end, since that which is imperfect on account of a failing in the chief act, is only in the wicked. . . .

The virtues must needs be connected together, so that whoever has one has all. Now whoever has grace has charity, so that he must needs have all the other virtues, and hence, since prudence is a virtue, he must, of necessity, have prudence also.

FROM QUESTION 49

We must now consider each quasi-integral part of prudence, and under this head there are eight points of inquiry: (1) Memory; (2) Understanding or Intelligence; (3) Docility; (4) Shrewdness; (5) Reason; (6) Foresight; (7) Circumspection; (8) Caution. . . .

Memory

Prudence regards contingent matters of action. Now in such like matters a man can be directed, not by those things that are simply and necessarily true, but by those which occur in the majority of cases: because principles must be proportionate to their conclusions, and *like must be concluded from like* (*Ethic.* vi). But we need experience to discover what is true in the majority of cases: wherefore the Philosopher [Aristotle] says (*Ethic.* ii. 1) that *intellectual virtue is engendered and fostered by experience and time.* Now experience is the result of many memories as stated in *Metaph.* i. 1, and therefore prudence requires the memory of many things. Hence memory is fittingly accounted a part of prudence.

Prudence applies universal knowledge to particulars which are objects of sense: hence many things belonging to the sensitive faculties are requisite for prudence, and memory is one of them.

Just as aptitude for prudence is in our nature, while its perfection comes through practice or grace, so too, as Tully says in his *Rhetoric*, memory not only arises from nature but is also aided by art and diligence.

Understanding

Understanding denotes here, not the intellectual power, but the right estimate about some final principle, which is taken as self-evident: thus we are said to understand the first principles of demonstrations. Now every deduction of reason proceeds from certain statements which are taken as primary: wherefore every process of reasoning must needs proceed from some understanding. Therefore since prudence is right reason applied to action, the whole process of prudence must needs have its source in understanding. Hence it is that understanding is reckoned a part of prudence.

The reasoning of prudence terminates, as in a conclusion, in the particular matter of action, to which it applies the knowledge of some universal principle. Now a singular conclusion is argued from a universal and a singular proposition.

Wherefore the reasoning of prudence must proceed from a twofold understanding. The one is cognizant of universals, and this belongs to the understanding which is an intellectual virtue, whereby we know naturally not only speculative principles but also practical universal principles, such as *One should do evil to no man.* The other understanding, as stated in *Ethic.* vi. 11, is cognizant of an extreme, i.e., of some primary singular and contingent practical matter, viz., the minor premise, which must needs be singular in the syllogism of prudence. Now this primary singular is some singular end, as stated in the same place. Wherefore the understanding which is a part of prudence is a right estimate of some particular end.

Docility

Prudence is concerned with particular matters of action, and since such matters are of infinite variety, no one man can consider them all sufficiently; nor can this be done quickly, for it requires length of time. Hence in matters of prudence man stands in very great need of being taught by others, especially by old folk who have acquired a sane understanding of the ends in practical matters. Wherefore the Philosopher [Aristotle] says (*Ethic.* vi. 11): *It is right to pay no less attention to the undemonstrated assertions and opinions of such persons as are experienced, older than we are, and prudent, than to their demonstrations, for their experience gives them an insight into principles.* Thus it is written (Prov. iii. 5): *Lean not on thy own prudence,* and (Ecclus. vi. 35): *Stand in the multitude of the ancients* (i.e., the old men), *that are wise, and join thyself from thy heart to their wisdom.* Now it is a mark of docility to be ready to be taught: and consequently docility is fittingly reckoned a part of prudence.

Although docility is useful for every intellectual virtue, yet it belongs to prudence chiefly.

Man has a natural aptitude for docility even as for other

things connected with prudence. Yet his own efforts count for much toward the attainment of perfect docility: and he must carefully, frequently and reverently apply his mind to the teachings of the learned, neither neglecting them through laziness, nor despising them through pride.

By prudence man makes precepts not only for others but also for himself. . . . And yet even the learned should be docile in some respects, since no man is altogether self-sufficient in matters of prudence.

Shrewdness

Prudence consists in a right estimate about matters of action. Now a right estimate or opinion is acquired in two ways, both in practical and in speculative matters, first by discovering it oneself, secondly by learning it from others. Now just as docility consists in a man being well disposed to acquire a right opinion from another man, so shrewdness is an apt disposition to acquire a right estimate by oneself, yet so that shrewdness be taken for *eustochia*, of which it is a part. For *eustochia* is a happy conjecture about any matter, while shrewdness is *an easy and rapid conjecture in finding the middle term* (*Poster.* i. 34). Nevertheless the philosopher [Andronicus] who calls shrewdness a part of prudence, takes it for *eustochia*, in general, hence he says: *Shrewdness is a habit whereby congruities are discovered rapidly*.

Reason

The work of prudence is to take good counsel, as stated in *Ethic.* vi. 7. Now counsel is a research proceeding from certain things to others. But this is the work of reason. Wherefore it is requisite for prudence that man should be an apt reasoner. And since the things required for the perfection of prudence are called requisite or quasi-integral parts of prudence, it follows that reason should be numbered among these parts.

Reason denotes here, not the power of reason, but its good use.

The certitude of reason comes from the intellect. Yet the need of reason is from a defect in the intellect, since those things in which the intellective power is in full vigor have no need for reason, for they comprehend the truth by their simple insight, as do God and the angels. On the other hand particular matters of action, wherein prudence guides, are very far from the condition of things intelligible, and so much the farther, as they are less certain and fixed. Thus matters of art, though they are singular, are nevertheless more fixed and certain, wherefore in many of them there is no room for counsel on account of their certitude, as stated in *Ethic.* iii. 3. Hence, although in certain other intellectual virtues reason is more certain than in prudence, yet prudence above all requires that man be an apt reasoner, so that he may rightly apply universals to particulars, which latter are various and uncertain.

Foresight

Prudence is properly about the means to an end, and its proper work is to set them in due order to the end. And although certain things are necessary for an end, which are subject to divine providence, yet nothing is subject to human providence except the contingent matters of actions which can be done by man for an end. Now the past has become a kind of necessity, since what has been done cannot be undone. In like manner, the present as such has a kind of necessity, since it is necessary that Socrates sit, so long as he sits.

Consequently, future contingents, insofar as they can be directed by man to the end of human life, are the matter of prudence: and each of these things is implied in the word foresight, for it implies the notion of something distant, to which that which occurs in the present has to be directed. Therefore foresight is part of prudence.

Whenever many things are requisite for a unity, one of them must needs be the principal to which all the others are subordinate. Hence in every whole one part must be formal and predominant, whence the whole has unity. Accordingly foresight is the principal of all the parts of prudence, since whatever else is required for prudence, is necessary precisely that some particular thing may be rightly directed to its end. Hence it is that the very name of prudence is taken from foresight (*providentia*) as from its principal part.

Speculation is about universal and necessary things, which, in themselves, are not distant, since they are everywhere and always, though they are distant from us, insofar as we fail to know them. Hence foresight does not apply properly to speculative but only to practical matters.

Right order to an end which is included in the notion of foresight, contains rectitude of counsel, judgment and command, without which no right order to the end is possible.

Circumspection

It belongs to prudence chiefly to direct something aright to an end; and this is not done aright unless both the end be good, and the means good and suitable.

Since, however, prudence is about singular matters of action, which contain many combinations of circumstances, it happens that a thing is good in itself and suitable to the end, and nevertheless becomes evil or unsuitable to the end, by reason of some combination of circumstances. Thus to show signs of love to someone seems, considered in itself, to be a fitting way to arouse love in his heart, yet if pride or suspicion of flattery arise in his heart, it will no longer be a means suitable to the end. Hence the need of circumspection in prudence, viz., of comparing the means with the circumstances.

Though the number of possible circumstances be infinite, the number of actual circumstances is not; and the judgment of reason in matters of action is influenced by things which are few in number.

Circumstances are the concern of prudence, because prudence has to fix them; on the other hand they are the concern of moral virtues, insofar as moral virtues are perfected by the fixing of circumstances.

Just as it belongs to foresight to look on that which is by its nature suitable to an end, so it belongs to circumspection to consider whether it be suitable to the end in view of the circumstances. Now each of these presents a difficulty of its own, and therefore each is reckoned a distinct part of prudence.

Caution

The things with which prudence is concerned are contingent matters of action, wherein, even as false is found with true, so is evil mingled with good, on account of the great variety of these matters of action, wherein good is often hindered by evil, and evil has the appearance of good. Wherefore prudence needs caution, so that we may have such a grasp of good as to avoid evil.

Caution is required in moral acts, that we may be on our guard, not against acts of virtue, but against the hindrance of acts of virtue.

It is the same in idea, to ensue good and to avoid the opposite evil, but the avoidance of outward hindrances is different in idea. Hence caution differs from foresight, although they both belong to the one virtue of prudence.

Of the evils which man has to avoid, some are of frequent occurrence; the like can be grasped by reason, and against them caution is directed, either that they may be avoided altogether, or that they may do less harm. Others there are that occur rarely and by chance, and these, since they are infinite in number, cannot be grasped by reason, nor is man able to take precautions against them, although by exercising prudence he is able to prepare against all the surprises of chance, so as to suffer less harm thereby.

Appendix

Conference Participants

The conference upon which this book is based, "Is the Bible Enough? Evangelicals, Prudence, and Foreign Policy," took place in Washington, D.C., November 7–8, 1991. The following twenty-five persons participated:

Lawrence Adams, Institute on Religion and Democracy
Mark Amstutz, Wheaton College
Doug Bandow, CATO Institute and syndicated columnist
Alberto R. Coll, Department of Defense
Michael Cromartie, Ethics and Public Policy Center
Dean C. Curry, Messiah College
James Finn, Freedom House
Daniel Heimbach, Department of the Navy
Roland Hoksbergen, Calvin College
Ronald Kirkemo, Point Loma Nazarene College
Chris Lamb, Department of Defense
Richard D. Land, Christian Life Commission,
    Southern Baptist Convention
Luis E. Lugo, Calvin College
Udo Middelmann, King's College, New York
Kenneth Myers, *Stewardship Journal*
Brian O'Connell, National Association of Evangelicals
Leonidas Pantelides, Embassy of Cyprus
Robert Royal, Ethics and Public Policy Center
Herbert Schlossberg, Fieldstead Institute

Amy Sherman, University of Virginia
James W. Skillen, Center for Public Justice
William Stevenson, Calvin College
George Weigel, Ethics and Public Policy Center
Chris Woehr, *News Network International*
Nicholas Wolterstorff, Yale Divinity School

Notes

Chapter 1

ALBERTO R. COLL

1. Josef Pieper, *The Four Cardinal Virtues* (Notre Dame, Ind.: University of Notre Dame Press, 1966), 21.
2. Aristotle, *Nichomachean Ethics*, VI, 1140b, 6–11.
3. Ibid., VI, 1142b, 32–35.
4. Ibid., V, 1137b–1138a.
5. Ibid., VI, 1141b, 15.
6. Ibid., VI, 1144a, 35–7.
7. Ibid., VI, 1144a, 6–31.
8. Ibid., VI, 1144b, 30–33.
9. Ibid., VI, 1145a, 6–11.
10. Thomas Aquinas, *Summa Theologiae*, 2a2ae. 49, 7.
11. Ibid., 2a2ae. 49, 1.
12. Ibid., 2a2ae. 49, 2. As he explained: "The reasoning involved in prudence draws on a double understanding. One, the understanding of general principles, which is for that understanding which is classed as an intellectual virtue; it is a habit of mind whereby by nature we see general principles, not only of theory but of practice as well, such as, *Do evil to nobody*. . . . The other understanding is . . . seeing the ultimate particular or factual principle. . . . This individual principle . . . is about an individual end. And so the understanding which is taken as part of prudence is a certain correct appreciation of some particular end."
13. Ibid., 2a2ae. 49, 3.
14. Ibid., 2a2ae. 49, 4.
15. Ibid., 2a2ae. 49, 5.
16. See the discussion in Pieper, *Four Cardinal Virtues*, 14–18.
17. *Summa Theologiae*, 2a2ae. 49, 7.
18. Ibid., 2a2ae. 49, 8.
19. Ibid., 1a2ae. 57, 4; 2a2ae. 50, 1.
20. Victoria Kahn, *Rhetoric, Prudence and Skepticism in the Renaissance* (Ithaca, N.Y.: Cornell University Press, 1985).
21. Leo Strauss, *Thoughts on Machiavelli* (Glencoe, Ill.: The Free Press,

1958); Eugene Garver, *Machiavelli and the History of Prudence* (Madison: University of Wisconsin Press, 1987).

22. Speech delivered on 11 May 1792. For the intellectual context of Burke's thought, see J. G. A. Pockock, *The Machiavellian Moment: Florentine Political Thought and the Atlantic Republican Tradition* (Princeton: Princeton University Press, 1975); Francis Canavan, *The Political Reason of Edmund Burke* (Durham, N.C.: Duke University Press, 1960).

23. Second letter to Sir Hercules Langrishe, IV, 57.

24. For an excellent discussion of the problematic nature of this effort, see the excellent discussion by Harvey Mansfield, "Edmund Burke," in *History of Political Philosophy*, 3d ed., ed. Leo Strauss and Joseph Cropsey (Chicago: University of Chicago Press, 1987), 692–695.

25. Ibid., 693.

26. First letter to Sir Hercules Langrishe, III, 304, cited in Gerald W. Chapman, *Edmund Burke: The Practical Imagination* (Cambridge: Harvard University Press, 1967), 138. Deeply aware of the fiercely competitive relationship among the numerous moral claims on the statesman's resources and commitments, Burke also counseled in this letter: "He forms the best judgment in all moral disquisitions, who has the greatest number and variety of considerations in one view before him, and can take them in with the best possible consideration of the middle results of all."

27. See, for example, Kenneth W. Thompson's discussion of prudence in *Morality and Foreign Policy* (Baton Rouge: Louisiana State University Press, 1980). In this and other works, Thompson also has emphasized the centrality to prudence and to sound statecraft of moral reasoning, which he defines in categories not foreign to Aquinas's own definition.

28. See the discussion in Clark E. Cochran, "The Radical Gospel and Christian Prudence," in *The Ethical Dimension of Political Life: Essays in Honor of John H. Hallowell*, ed. Francis Canavan (Durham, N.C.: Duke University Press, 1983), 188–99.

29. Reinhold Niebuhr, *Moral Man and Immoral Society* (New York: Charles Scribner's Sons, 1960), 83–112.

30. *New Catholic Encyclopedia* (New York: McGraw-Hill, 1967), 11:928, col. 2, cited in Cochran, "Radical Gospel," 196.

31. See Niebuhr's closing words in *The Children of Light and the Children of Darkness* (New York: Charles Scribner's Sons, 1944), 188–90.

32. Cited in Thompson, *Morality and Foreign Policy*, 143.

Chapter 2

JAMES FINN

1. Dean Acheson, "Ethics in International Relations Today," *Amherst Alumni News*, Winter 1965, 2.

2. Ibid. 2–3.

3. Hans Morgenthau, "The Demands of Prudence," *Worldview*, June 1960, 6.

4. George F. Kennan, "Morality and Foreign Policy," *Foreign Affairs*, Winter 1985–86, 206.

5. *Pacem in Terris* (New York: Paulist Press, 1963), para. 7.

6. Charles Krauthammer, "The Reagan Doctrine," *Intervention & the Reagan Doctrine* (New York: Council on Religion and International Affairs, 1985), 23.

7. For this statistic and subsequent information on aid to Africa, I am indebted to "When Foreign Aid Fails" by Jack Shepard, *The Atlantic Monthly*, April 1985, 41–46; and to "Why Can't Africa Feed Itself?" by George B. N. Ayittey, *International Health & Development*, Summer 1989, 18–21.

8. Robert M. Gates gave extended testimony before the Senate Select Committee on Intelligence on 3–4 October 1991. The excerpts quoted were transcribed by the Federal Information Systems Corporation, a private transcription service, and published by the *New York Times*.

9. Raymond Aron, *Peace and War: A Theory of International Relations* (Garden City, N.Y.: Doubleday & Company, 1966), 585.

10. Josef Pieper, *Prudence* (New York: Pantheon, 1959), 54, 67.

Chapter 3

Luis E. Lugo

1. C. S. Lewis, *The Four Loves* (New York: Harcourt, Brace, 1960), 47–48.

2. Alan Tonelson, "What Is the National Interest?" *The Atlantic Monthly*, July 1991, 39.

3. See Doug Bandow, "Foreign Policy and Limited Government: Keep the Troops and the Money at Home," *Orbis*, Fall 1991, 549–61.

4. Cited in Bernice Hamilton, *Political Thought in Sixteenth-Century Spain* (Oxford: Claredon Press, 1963), 109.

5. Jeanne Kirkpatrick, "Dictatorships and Double Standards," *Commentary*, November 1979, 34–45.

6. Charles Krauthammer, "Morality and the Reagan Doctrine," *The New Republic*, 8 September 1986, 24.

7. Hedley Bull, "The State's Positive Role in World Affairs," *Daedalus* 108 (Fall 1979): 123.

8. Richard Weaver, "Lord Acton: The Historian as Thinker," *Modern Age*, Winter 1960–61, 15, 21.

9. See Alexis de Tocqueville, *Democracy in America*, vol. 2, book 4, chap. 6.

Index of Names

131